classic herman miller

leslie piña

4880 Lower Valley Road, Atglen, PA 19310

dedicated to those who have
given us modern classics

Piña, Leslie A., 1947-
    Classic Herman Miller / Leslie Piña.
        p.   cm.
    Includes bibliographical references and index.
    ISBN 0-7643-0471-2
    1. Herman Miller (Firm)--Catalogs. 2. Furniture--United States--History--20th
century--Catalogs.   I. Title
NK2439.H42A4   1998
749.213--dc21   97-41179
                                                            CIP

ISBN: 0-7643-0471-2
Book design by Leslie Piña
Book layout by Blair Loughrey

Printed in China

Published by Schiffer Publishing Ltd.
4880 Lower Valley Road
Atglen, PA 19310
Phone: (610) 593-1777; Fax: (610) 593-2002
E-mail: Info@schifferbooks.com
Please visit our web site catalog at
www.schifferbooks.com

This book may be purchased from the publisher.
Include $3.95 for shipping. Please try your bookstore first.
We are always looking for people to write books on new and
related subjects. If you have an idea for a book please contact
us at the above address.
You may write for a free catalog.

In Europe, Schiffer books are distributed by
Bushwood Books
6 Marksbury Avenue
Kew Gardens
Surrey TW9 4JF England
Phone: 44 (0) 20-8392-8585; Fax: 44 (0) 20-8392-9876
E-mail: info@bushwoodbooks.co.uk
Free postage in the UK. Europe: air mail at cost.

Acknowledgments

It follows that a company with a strong sense of identity and image would have a clear view of its past, a conscious posture toward its future, and good archives. At Herman Miller, the archive collection is awesome, and I am grateful for the privilege of using it. All photographs and illustrations in this book are from the archives. Bob Viol, the Corporate Archivist, is a gem, and I would like to acknowledge his generosity in sharing his expertise, providing assistance with this project, and extending hospitality during our visits. Thanks Bob! I am also grateful to Archive Assistant Gloria Laarman and Project Manager Rich Rutledge at Herman Miller for their kindness and assistance.

Thanks to the interlibrary loan system, to the Michigan Interstate Highways for having a 70 mph speed limit, to Ramón for his help at the archives, to Bob Viol and Paula Ockner for proofreading, to Peter Schiffer for his friendship and sense of humor, and to the staff at Schiffer Publishing.

Classic Herman Miller

Contents

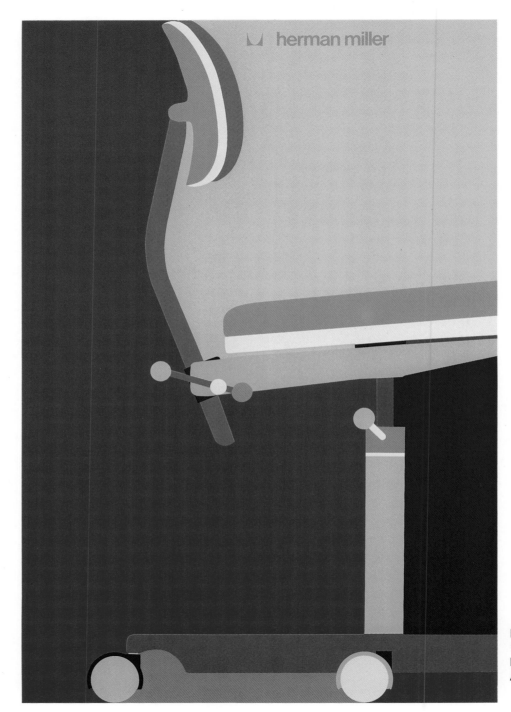

MKD Chair in
1977 graphic
by artist Per
Arnoldi.

Introduction

I used to work at home on an uncomfortable old chair, probably from a dining set, in front of a 1950s blond wood desk that did not accommodate a computer and keyboard. It is too difficult to part with the desk, but I recently brought home an Eames Soft Pad Chair with polished aluminum arms and frame, cushioned leather upholstery, a seat with adjustable height that tilts back and swivels, and a sturdy four-pronged pedestal with wheels (I also discovered an ingenious keyboard stand called a Scooter). My husband Ramón looked at the chair, sat down, stood up, sat down again and said, "This is a wonderful desk chair." Then he looked at it again and added, "It's also beautiful. We could use it just as well in the family room or even the living room." (He probably forgot that the living room is never used, except occasionally as a cut-through). Then it hit me why the chair was considered a classic and why it is included in a very distinctive catalog of the "Herman Miller for the Home" line of furnishings.

The perception of designers, manufacturers, dealers, and other people who talk about furniture is that there are two disparate categories — contract and residential. Contract furniture is for the workplace and public places away from home; residential furniture, as the name denotes, is for the home. In other words, one is for places where people work, and the other is for places where people live. In the United States (more than in Europe) there is little crossover. To keep this segregation clear, even the styles differ. For the most part, twentieth-century residential furniture has been, and still is, based on historic styles. Even as we approach the threshold of the millennium, it is no more surprising to see a room filled with uninspired wannabe eighteenth-century look-alikes than it is to see state-of-the-art

electronics perched on them. Americans have an uncanny capacity for accepting visual and cultural anomalies.

Modernism, the creation of new forms with a conscious effort to avoid historic style and redundant ornament, has found wider acceptance in the area of contract furniture than residential. Even in the early twentieth-century, office furniture, though basically without style, was designed to be utilitarian. The attempt at function was a carry-over from the mechanical inventions called "patent furniture" in the Victorian era, and it took precedence over style and decoration. After the Second World War, the really alert designers began to introduce inspired forms of truly functional furniture that even looked original. It was designed from the inside out, and it could be appreciated from the outside in. Plus, it could be mass produced and marketed for huge populations of people in the workplace who suddenly needed furniture to accommodate new ways of doing business and better systems for organizing information. Inspired by what had been perceived as a handful of pre-war tubular steel Bauhaus prototypes and other austere eccentricities, it was the beginning of a revolution. With super-designers and thinkers like George Nelson and Charles and Ray Eames on board, Herman Miller was suddenly in the process of reinventing itself and modern furniture. Then in 1968 with the debut of Robert Propst's Action Office, the first open office system with interchangeable components and extreme flexibility, the revolution was in full swing. But with few exceptions, the American home still looked about the same as it did before this rather radical reconfiguration of the American office.

Back cover of 1989 Herman Miller Magazine, showing Capella, Hollington, Equa, and Ergon chairs.

Front cover.

Family of company leaders: Max, D. J., and Hugh De Pree.

Today, neither the retail residential furniture industry nor the ubiquitous blandness of the American home have changed significantly. What is really curious is the division between work place and living place. Don't people in fact live where they work and also work where they live? Most workers spend about one third of their day, maybe a fourth of their lives, in the workplace. Most of the other three fourths is spent at home (including sleep time). When these two worlds are taken together, we live most of our lives with furniture. We eat on it, write on it, place things on it, work at it, and store things in it and on it. We decorate with it, put our feet up on it, lose things in its crevices, and watch the cat jump on it. We sit, lounge, play, make love, sleep, give birth, and die on it. Furniture is as much a part of our lives as any material object can be. Yet we casually allow others to design, build, and even select it for us without batting an eye. Most people give little thought to, or have little say in, the posture of their backs or the pleasure of their spirits. They are more particular about details when ordering a meal than in choosing a chair that will support a species-specific weak back and give comfort to a hyper-sedentary bottom for years, perhaps decades.

So why not have well-designed, functional, comfortable, durable, and good-looking furniture in both the workplace and the residence? And if it happens to have modern styling consistent with a modern lifestyle, why should it be limited to the office or workplace? These are

questions that the people at Herman Miller have been asking for years, and in 1994 they introduced a line of mid-century classics plus new designs called "Herman Miller for the Home." Although these classics have been perceived primarily as contract furniture, they have also been attracting the attention of a growing cult of modernism collectors, dealers, and a general audience that is noticing the lack of style and choice in the residential marketplace. The great designs are classics because they are still great by any standard. The company that led the office revolution has become a classic in its own right for acting on its beliefs and good ideas. Softening the barrier between contract and residential furniture is one of these ideas, and the classics, like the Soft Pad Chair in my home, are candidates for the job.

The Star Furniture Co. was founded in Zeeland, Michigan in 1905 to produce high quality furniture, especially bedroom suites, in historic revival styles. Dirk Jan De Pree began as a clerk with the company in 1909 and became its president by 1919, when it was renamed the Michigan Star Furniture Co. De Pree and his father-in-law, Herman Miller purchased 51% of the stock in 1923 and renamed the company Herman Miller Furniture Co. In 1960 it became Herman Miller, Inc.

Until 1930 the company produced only traditional wood furniture. With the shrinking market of the Depression, they hired Gilbert Rohde and reluctantly took a chance with modern design. Rohde helped turn the company

Vintage furniture display in Chicago Showroom at NeoCon in 1985, showing
Eames Fiberglass Armshell and RAR Rocker, Elliptical (Surfboard) Table, Wire
Base Table, and Sofa Compact with Girard fabric; photo 1985 *by Bill Lindhout.*

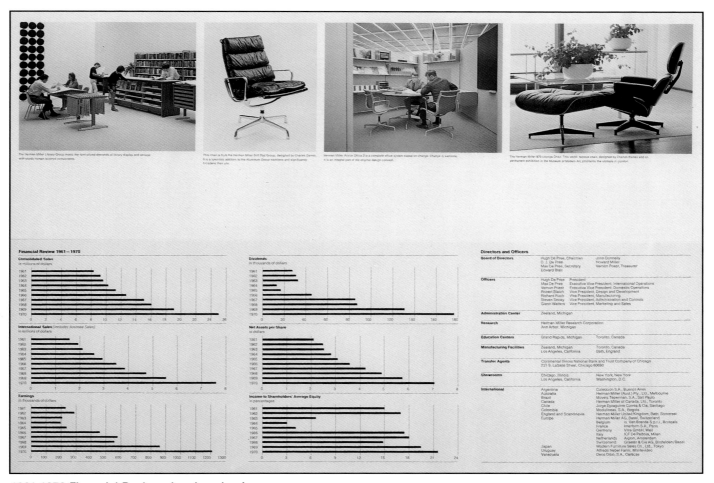

1961-1970 Financial Review showing classics.

in a totally new direction, and in 1933 its modern furniture debut was held at the Century of Progress exposition in Chicago. A showroom in the Chicago Merchandise Mart opened in 1939, and another opened in New York in 1941. Herman Miller entered the office furniture market in 1942 with its modular Executive Office Group (EOG) system designed by Rohde. When Rohde died in 1944 his replacement was architect George Nelson, who joined Herman Miller as director of design in 1945 and carried on with the EOG concept. In addition to Nelson's enormous personal contribution over the next four decades, he helped recruit other designers: Isamu Noguchi, who is known for his Biomorphic coffee table of 1947; Charles and Ray Eames among whose many contributions are series of molded plywood and molded plastic furniture that set the standard for modern furniture design; Alexander Girard, who designed vibrant textiles and bold graphics. Another important name is Robert Propst, head of Herman Miller Research Division formed in 1960, and inventor of the Action Office. Designs for Action Office I (1964-1970) were by the George Nelson office.

Herman Miller Sets High Expectations for Service

The Herman Miller Promise℠ is a commitment to customers that springs from the company's total confidence in the quality and lasting value of its products. And The Promise℠ sets a published standard of guaranteed service unmatched in the office furniture industry.

Herman Miller promises every customer, large or small:

- **A five-year product warranty.** Whether you buy a single chair or 100 workstations, Herman Miller guarantees the same commitment to customer satisfaction.
- **Quality audits after project installation.** Herman Miller stands by you long after the sale. As your long-term partner, the company follows up to assure that your installation provides the performance you expect.
- **Trade-in allowances on systems products.** A 20-percent trade-in value sets the Action Office® and Action Office Encore™ systems apart in the industry. The 100-percent trade-in value on Ethospace® frames shows what makes the Ethospace tile-and-frame construction unique: The frames don't become obsolete. By trading frames for larger or smaller sizes, facility changes can be made with minimal additional costs.
- **Guaranteed move-in dates.** Herman Miller's commitment to on-time delivery and installation allays a major fear among customers who've been burned before.

This unprecedented package remains the industry's most comprehensive guarantee of customer satisfaction. It's your written assurance of support and another reason to feel confident in your decision to purchase Herman Miller products.

Herman Miller "promise" button and article in Herman Miller Magazine, 1987.

Although many of the original mid-century classics and those reissued as part of the Herman Miller for the Home collection have been used in residences, the focus of Herman Miller has been, and is today, on modern office environments. A new group of designers, including Don Chadwick, Bruce Burdick, Bill Stumpf, and Geoff Hollington have addressed the needs of both home and office environments, and their contributions are likely to become the classics of the future. The values have not changed; belief in the importance of good design, honest products, and respect for individuals and the environment have been, and continue to be, driving forces. The Herman Miller philosophy states, "We are committed to quality and excellence in all that we do and the way in which we do it." The quality and excellence begins with a need that is followed by a design. As former president (son of D.J.) Hugh De Pree said, "If there is anything that distinguishes Herman Miller from most other companies, it is our faith in the efficacy of design" (De Pree 27). The classics that are presented here are testimony to that faith.

Part One

Designers of mid-century classics in the 1994 Herman Miller for the Home Catalog.

Chapter 1

Charles and Ray Eames

Charles and Ray
Eames, c. 1975;
*photo by Charles
Eames.*

Charles Ormand Eames (1907-1978)

Born in St. Louis, Missouri, Charles Eames went to work as a laborer in a steel mill at age fourteen. After working as a draftsman, he won a scholarship to study architecture at Washington University in St. Louis. He attended from 1925 to 1928, but allegedly flunked out because of his devotion to Frank Lloyd Wright. After marrying Catherine Dewey Woermann, he traveled in Europe in 1929. He was a partner in the architectural firm Gray and Eames (later with Pauly) in St. Louis from 1930-1933, and lived in Mexico in 1934. From 1934-1938 he was a partner in the firm Eames and Walsh. After studying at the Cranbrook Academy of Art on scholarship from 1938-1939, Eames taught at Cranbrook from 1939-1941, while also working for Eliel and Eero Saarinen.

In 1941 Eames divorced Catherine to marry Ray Kaiser. The couple moved to Los Angeles and developed new techniques for molding plywood. The new husband and wife partnership would be the source of significant modern design under the name "Offices of Charles and Ray Eames." He was awarded the Kaufmann International Design Award in 1961, an American Institute of Architects Award in 1977, and the Queen's Gold Medal for Architecture in London, posthumously, in 1979.

The Royal Gold Medal for Architecture is generally regarded as the premier international architectural award. It was instituted in 1848 by Queen Victoria and is conferred annually by the Sovereign on "some distinguished architect or group of architects, for work of high merit or on some distinguished person or persons whose work has promoted either directly or indirectly the advancement of architecture." Its presentation to Charles and Ray Eames was only the second time it had been awarded to a partnership.

Interiors magazine described him in the special 1965 anniversary issue: "He cares terribly for the human condition and his philosophy is simple: you do those things you believe in and avoid those which you do not" (130). Hugh De Pree wrote that Eames "had great personal discipline, was obsessed with quality and excellence, made outrageous demands on those who worked for and with him..." (47). Ralph Caplan said, "Charles Eames was not always teaching, but when you were with him you were always learning" (De Pree 50).

Ray Kaiser Eames (1912-1988)

Ray Kaiser was born in Sacramento, California. She attended the May Friend Bennett School in Millbrook, New Jersey from 1931-1933, and then the Art Students League in New York before studying painting at the Hans Hoffman School from 1933-1939. She attended Cranbrook Academy of Art from 1940-1941 and then married Charles Eames in 1941. Some of her work, such as designs for covers of *Art & Architecture* magazine in the early 1940s, was individual, but most of her work was in partnership with her husband in the Offices of Charles and Ray Eames from 1941-1978. After Charles died in 1978, she continued the work of what is considered to be one of the greatest husband and wife design collaborations of the century.

Offices of Charles and Ray Eames

After architect Charles Ormand Eames married artist Ray Kaiser, they formed a design partnership that became an important source of modern design from 1941 to 1978. From 1941-1942 they developed plywood splints for the United States Navy and formed the Plyformed Wood Co., which later became the Molded Plywood Division of Evans Products. They designed The Toy in 1951, House of Cards in 1952, and Giant House of Cards in 1953. For the 1964 New York World's Fair they designed the IBM Corp. Pavilion, Herman Miller showrooms, and other exhibits. Their work included graphics and houses as well as photography. From 1946-1978 they made many experimental and award-winning films. Architect and industrial designer Eliot Noyes said, "After the first Eames chair development right after World War II, no furniture anywhere in the world was being designed that wasn't influenced by it" (De Pree 47). Royalties from Eames furniture designs represented their greatest source of income over the years. By 1975 an estimated half billion dollars worth of their chairs had already been sold, with an average royalty of 1.5% of the net. In 1974 they received more than $15,000 per month in royalties. (*Fortune* 1975, 99)

The posthumous citation from the Royal Institute of British Architects read, "The nomination of the Eames Office for the 1979 RIBA Gold Medal pays tribute to its record of innovation and excellence in such diverse fields as architecture, furniture and, more recently, communication through the medium of films, graphics and exhibitions....Their furniture has become a byword and is in a well trodden path of architect-designed contemporary classics....Like the house, an abundance of possibilities, not too precious and never pompous. The vocabulary has proved rich enough to enable a new generation of designers to develop in their own right."

Evans Products Co., Molded Plywood Division

In 1941 Charles and Ray Eames and three colleagues established the Plyformed Wood Co. in West Los Angeles. After getting the United States Navy contract for plywood splints, the company moved to nearby Venice, California. In 1943 Edward S. Evans, head of Evans Products Co. in Detroit, bought the rights to produce and distribute the Plyformed Wood splints, and the company was renamed Molded Plywood Division, a subsidiary of Evans Products. Evans Products took over production of the splints, while the Molded Plywood Division experimented with other products, such as chairs and children's furniture in 1945.

When the Eameses' chairs and other plywood furniture were exhibited at the Museum of Modern Art, they attracted the attention of George Nelson and D.J. De Pree of Herman Miller. In 1947 Herman Miller gained exclusive rights to distribute the products. Then, the Venice plant closed and moved to Grand Haven, Michigan. In 1949 Herman Miller purchased the manufacturing rights for Eames chairs from Evans, and the manufacturing equipment was installed in Zeeland.

Eames Molded Plywood Furniture for Herman Miller

The molded plywood chair has been called "the most famous chair of the century," and it was recognized as "the symbol of modernism" by the International Designers Society of America at its "Worldesign" conference in 1985.

Various woods and materials were used to make molded plywood furniture. Identification of these materials may help to date these items:

Mahogany — c.1946-1948

Rosewood — c.1946-1948; reintroduced 1961-c.1966

Oak — only 1953

Avodire — c.1946-1948

Canaletta —c 1946-1947

Slunkskin — 1948-1953

Fabric — 1948-1953

Leather — 1948-1953

Yellow — c.1946-1948

Red — c 1946-1958

Black — c.1946-c.1966. The DCW Chairs were finished in black by impregnating them with resin during the molding process, making the finish an integral part of the wood.

Walnut — c.1946-1958; reintroduced 1962-c.1966

Birch — c.1946-1958

Calico ash c. 1946-c.1966

Zebrawood — 1958-1959

Teak — 1958-1961

In addition to being produced for a limited time, some finishes and materials were sold in very low numbers. In 1948 only 9 Yellow, 2 Rosewood, 21 Avodire, no Canaletta, and 8 Mahogany were sold, compared to over 600 each of walnut finish, calico ash, and birch. In 1949, of the 5,672 molded plywood chairs sold, only 9 were Slunkskin, 5 leather, and 91 with fabric, with about 1,000 each of walnut finish, calico ash, and birch, plus 719 black and 511 red.

The DCM (Dining Chair Metal) Chairs were always sold in much greater quantities than the LCM (originally called Low Chair Metal, but changed to Lounge Chair Metal) Chairs. For example, in 1950 about 9,000 DCMs were sold, compared to 3,000 LCMs. The largest number of plywood chairs sold was in 1952, with a total of 21,526, 18,000 of which were DCMs. In 1960 there were 2,300 DCMs to 260 LCMs sold; in 1966 9,577 DCMs to only 260 LCMs sold.

Abbreviations for Eames designs from the Herman Miller 1948 product catalog:

CTM: round coffee table, metal. 34" diameter, 15" high. Birch, walnut, calico ash, black, red.

CTW-1: oblong coffee table, wood. 24" x 35". 15-1/2" high. Birch legs, tops of walnut, birch or black Formica.

CTW-3: round coffee table, wood. 34" diameter, 15" high. Birch, walnut, calico ash, black, red.

DCM: dining chair, metal. 19-1/2" width; 28 3/4" back height; 20-3/4" base depth. Birch, walnut, calico ash, black, red.

DCW: dining chair, wood. 17-1/2" seat height; 28 3/4" back height; 22-1/4" base depth. Birch, walnut, calico ash, black, red.

DTM-1: dining table, metal. Equipped with folding legs. 34" x 54" top; 29-1/2" high.

DTM-2: card table or extension for DTM-1. 34" x 34"

DTW-1: dining table, wood, with detachable legs. 34" x 54" top; 29-1/2" high. Finishes birch, walnut, black.

DTW-2: card table or extension for DTW-1. 30" x 34"

FSW: folding screen, wood. Widths up to five feet. Finishes: birch, walnut, calico ash, black, red.

IT: incidental table. A miniature, only 18" x 21-1/2", and 17" high.

LCM: low chair, metal. 22-1/4" width; 15-1/2" seat height; 26-1/4" back height; 25" base depth

LCW: low chair, wood. 15-1/2" seat height; 26 1/4" back height; 24-1/4" base depth

Production dates of Eames furniture designs

Eames supplied Herman Miller with successful furniture designs for more than three decades, and many of these classics have been produced continuously or have been reintroduced:

Children's Chairs: 1946-1947

DCM (Dining Chair Metal): 1946-1971; became EC110 1971-present

LCM (Lounge Chair Metal): 1946-present

DCW (Dining Chair Wood): 1946-1953; reintroduced 1994

LCW (Lounge Chair Wood): 1946-1958; reintroduced 1994

CTM (Coffee Table Metal): 1948-1957

CTW (Coffee Table Wood): 1946-1953; reintroduced 1994

FSW (Folding Screen Wood): 1946-1956; reintroduced 1994

Storage units: 1950-1955; Desk: 1951-1955

DAX Molded Plastic Dining Armchair with legs: 1950-1989

LAX Lounge Armchair with legs: 1950-?

LAR Lounge Chair with cat-in-the-cradle wire base: 1950-1967

PAW Swivel chair with wood legs and metal bracing: 1952-1953

PKW Swivel desk chair with wood legs and metal bracing: 1952-1954

RAR Shell Armchair on rockers: 1950-1968; for employees becoming parents: 1968-1984

Wire Base Table: 1950-present

Elliptical Table: 1951-1964; reintroduced 1994

Wire Mesh Chairs: 1951-1953

Hang-It-All: 1953-1961; reintroduced 1994

Sofa Compact: 1954-present

Stacking Chair: 1955-present

Lounge Chair and Ottoman: 1956-present. Cushions down filled until 1979; upholstery in leather, naugahyde, or fabric from 1956-1962; only leather used from 1962 on. Rosewood veneer discontinued in 1990.

Aluminum Group Furniture: 1958-present. Contract Base used until Universal Base was added in 1968. In 1975 the finish on columns and tilt-swivels were changed from black to dark tone, and new casters were available on desk chairs.

Executive Seating: 1960-present

Walnut Stools: 1960-present

La Fonda Chair: 1961-1990

La Fonda Table: 1961-present

Contract storage: 1961-1970

Tandem Sling seating: 1962-present

Tandem Shell seating: 1963-c.1993

Segmented Base Tables: 1964-1965

Chaise: 1968-present

Soft Pad Group: 1968-present. In 1975 the finish on columns and tilt-swivels were changed from black to dark tone, and new casters were available on desk chairs. The four-star base changed to a five-star. Soft Pad Lounges and Ottomans added in 1973.

Loose Cushion Armchair: 1972-?

Marble Tables: 1973-present

2-Seat and 3-Seat Sofas (Soft Pad Sofas): 1984-present

Conversations with and about Eames

In a conversation with Harvard professor and Eames exhibition consultant Owen Gingerich, Charles Eames talked about his work.

On the chairs:

One of the things we had committed ourselves to was trying to do a chair with a hard surface that was as comfortable as it could be in relation to the human body and also that would be self-explanatory as you looked at it — no mysteries, so that the techniques of how it was mad would be part of the aesthetics. We felt very strongly about this, because at the time there were so many things made with the opposite idea in mind, that is, to disguise a thing as if it were made at the Gobelin factories in Paris, when in fact it had been manufactured by modern techniques. (Gingerich 328)

On patents:

Now what divides the patentable from the non-patentable is entirely different from what divides the good and appropriate from the bad and the inappropriate. If one has bitten the apple and been seduced into the idea of having a patentable item and royalties, there is always the temptation to make the design such as to be patentable rather than to be good....If the client wants to patent them, that's his problem...but we will not put any of our effort into twisting the thing so that it's patentable. (328)

On plagiarism:

What you really worry about in the design of furniture or in architecture are the *bad* copies, when your idea is used in a kind of booby way. You don't mind if someone carries your idea further in a better way, although at first your nose may be a bit out of joint. (329)

For years the Eameses' studio was in an unconverted automotive garage in Venice, California with "24-hour Towing Service" and "Fenders and Body Work" signs outside. Southern California and Western Michigan were at least as distant culturally as they were geographically at mid-century. A good illustration of this cultural diversity and indication of the risks Herman Miller often took, is provided by architect-writer Peter Blake in his delightful book *No Place Like Utopia.*

In 1959 the United States was planning its first presentation of American cultural achievement to the Soviet Union with the American Exhibition in Moscow's Sokolniki Park — like a mini-world's fair. The United States Information Agency appointed Jack Masey to direct the exhibition, who in turn selected George Nelson as the overall designer. Among the various components, Peter Blake designed an exhibit on modern American architecture, and Buckminster Fuller designed a 30,000-square-foot 250-foot diameter geodesic dome. Blake describes the planning:

All of us went to work in New York and elsewhere preparing the necessary drawings and models and all the rest. Considering the fact that those in charge — Jack, George, and an ever present company of Washington apparatchiks — were not exactly known for their seamless efficiency, the entire operation went almost like clockwork. Jack was on the verge of a permanent nervous breakdown, as usual, and for various uninteresting reasons; George was between marriages, and hence, for some reason, permanently becalmed; Bucky was happily designing his...dome; and the Washington apparatchiks were being helpful by writing memos, sending out forms, and holding meetings at which nothing was decided. The situation, in short, was normal. Our work progressed (229).

One problem that needed a solution was filling the huge dome, so Charles and Ray Eames, who had already earned a reputation for molded plastic and plywood furniture, were invited to fill it. The Eameses had been developing experimental documentary films, and they planned to portray "a day in the life of the United States" in a multiple-projection film called "Glimpses of the U.S.A." This would be projected simultaneously on seven 20 x 30 foot screens, and it would run throughout each day. Blake explains:

> Charles and Ray Eames were hardly in the mainstream of American culture. They were very much "on the cutting edge"; and for a staid U.S. government agency to commission two such unpredictable experimenters to produce what was to be the theme song of our exhibition was mind-boggling....Nobody had a very clear idea of what Charles and Ray were going to produce. Charles had an incoherent semi-stammer that communicated little except his own boundless enthusiasm, and his incoherent "explanations" of whatever it was that excited him most at any given moment were punctuated by Ray's shrill giggles, designed to second her husband's enthusiastic double-talk.

At one of the Washington meetings that "take the place of thought and action," Charles Eames was invited to participate. He appeared "in California garb with Leicas dangling from his neck, and proceeded to jump on the conference room table to snap pictures..." Needless to say, no agenda was observed, and no minutes were taken at what had been intended as a typical bureaucratic briefing session (230).

Masey and Nelson commuted back and forth between Washington and Moscow as the exhibit took form. It looked as if they would meet their deadline, the huge dome was built, and the seven huge screens were mounted and ready for Eameses' films. Neither the Eameses nor the films were in sight, and the others were "beginning to have a collective nervous breakdown." Then just forty-eight hours before show time,

> ...the two of them walked out of the dark of Sokolniki Park and straight into Bucky's dome. They were dressed in...wrinkled camping togs and over-the-shoulder-bags containing seven reels of film, in cans. The Eameses were beaming from ear to ear — and if we hadn't been so relieved, we probably would have wrung their necks. Charles went up to the projectors, checked them out, inserted the reels, and flicked the various switches. And on the seven screens, projected precisely and in total synch, appeared a multimedia show that was, quite simply, flawless (241).

The Eameses had not only produced a technical and creative masterpiece in a medium that they were still in the process of inventing, they had never even seen the actual setting before that day. The entire production process had taken place in their little studio in Venice, California. With this picture of the designers in mind, it is understandable that they never chose to take up residence in Zeeland, Michigan near Herman Miller. Yet they continued to have a symbiotic relationship in which both the designers and the company reaped great rewards — in dollars, in notoriety, and in the unparalleled contribution to twentieth-century American design.

Shortly after the Moscow exhibit, Charles Eames was interviewed on film about his design philosophy. The following excerpts are from *Business As Unusual* (61-64):

What are the boundaries of design?
Eames: What are the boundaries of problems?

Are there tendencies and schools of design?

Eames: Yes, but these are more a measure of human limitations than of ideals.

Ought design tend toward the ephemeral or toward permanence?

Eames: Those needs and designs that have a more universal quality tend toward relative permanence.

Have you been forced to accept compromises?

Eames: I don't remember ever being forced to accept compromises, but I have willingly accepted constraints.

Does design obey laws?
Aren't constraints enough?

Charles Eames was also interviewed for the November 1965 issue of *Interiors* magazine in an article entitled, "25: Year of Appraisal." The previous twenty-five years had seen the field of interior design develop out of the former "dilettante's hobby," interior decorating. Leading designers, such as Charles Eames, were asked to comment on the state of design in 1965.

Eames on design:

Any questions — thus any answers — are tempered by the time of life they are asked — whatever cycle you are in at the time... After a decade of neat, beautiful rectilinear drawings and somebody shows you squiggles, you fall upon squiggles as the answer to the world. (130)

On affluence:

Affluence offers the kind of freedom I am deeply suspicious of. It offers freedom from restraint, and it is virtually impossible to do something without restraints. If you look through history at the greatest things of all times, the greatest were produced where the conditions of restraint were so great that there was relatively little choice...(130)

On freedom and technology:

...the freedom is like a hurricane. It becomes not a question of what we are doing with [it] — it is the appalling fact of what *it* is doing with us. (131)

On freedom, affluence, and design:

Freedom and affluence usually mean freedom to do any imaginable amount of ugliness...Example: the program for designing either an oil cracking plant or jet transport would consist of a great list of functional and economic restraints — and the probability of a good and handsome result would be high. The program for designing a monument or a world's fair pavilion which would reflect freedom and affluence would have a low probability of a great solution...Los Angeles is an example of a city built without restraints. (131-32)

Some of the following examples of Herman Miller furniture designed by Charles and Ray Eames have been discontinued, while others have either been produced continuously or have been recently reintroduced in the Herman Miller for the Home line. Each was designed with the right balance of freedom and restraint. Both Herman Miller's and the Eameses' sensitivity to materials, technologies, human comfort, and aesthetics have insured that these designs would become, and remain, modern classics.

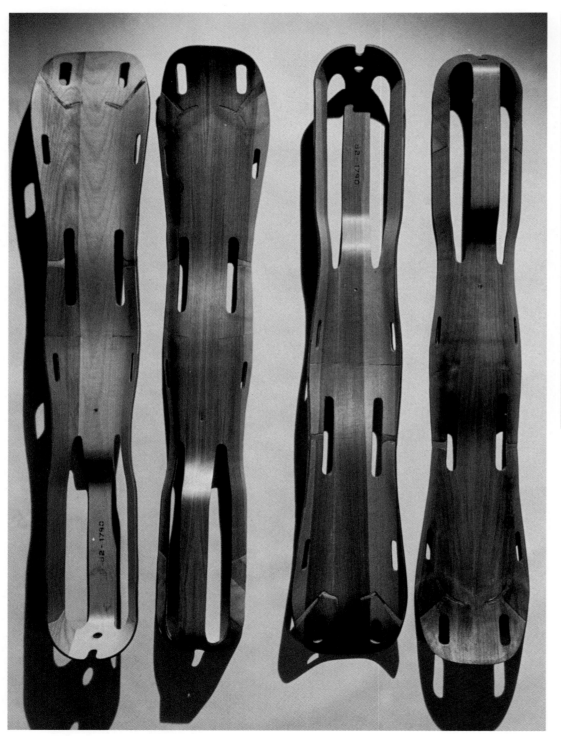

Above:
Prototype of three-legged
molded plywood chair; photo
1943 *by Charles Eames.*

Left:
Front and back view of Eames
molded plywood splints,
commissioned by the United
States Navy in 1942; photo
1945 *by Charles Eames.*

Opposite:
Three Eames Molded Plywood
Chairs and a Molded Plywood
Table and Stool; photo 1946 *by
Charles Eames.*

Bottom of DCM Chair, designed in 1946 of five-ply molded plywood, hardwood inner plies, light ash face veneers, bright chrome-plated steel rod base and back brace, rubber shocks, nylon glides; photo 1959 *by Earl Woods.*

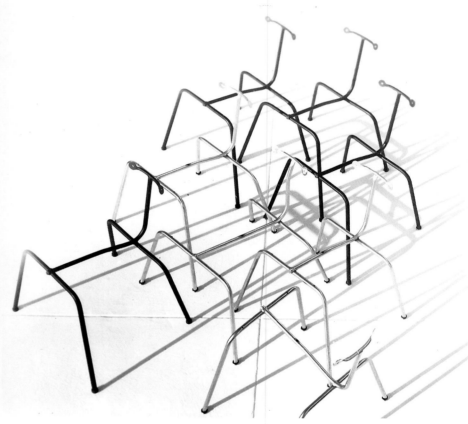

Chrome-plated steel rod frames for DCM Chairs.

Top left:
Back support for LCW or
DCW Chair; photo 1946 *by
Charles Eames.*

Top right:
Piece of molded plywood
used in prototype chair;
photo 1946 *by Charles
Eames.*

Right:
Prototype of chair back,
front and side view; photo
1946 by Charles Eames.

Children's Molded Plywood Table, Chairs, and Stools; the 1946-1947 trial run of about 5,000 pieces was not a commercial success, so the items were discontinued; since children's furniture generally does not hold up well, the items are rarely found; photo 1945 *by Charles Eames.*

Six Molded Plywood Children's Tables
stacked; photo 1946 *by Charles Eames.*

Two Molded Plywood Children's Chairs with heart cutouts; photo 1975.

Original Eames molded plywood chair; photo 1946.

Original Eames molded plywood chair; photo 1946.

Opposite:
Red painted Molded
Plywood DCW and
LCW Chairs; photo
1981 *by Bill Sharpe.*

EC110 and LCM Chairs in various new finishes; photo 1989 *by Bill Sharpe*.

Grouping of Molded Plywood Chairs and Tables with
Herman Miller logo; photo 1946 *by Charles Eames.*

Above left:
LCM Chair with slunk skin; photo
1950 *by Charles Eames.*

Above right:
Group of Molded Plywood and
Fiberglass Chairs in a parking lot;
photo 1950 *by Charles Eames.*

Left:
Molded Plywood Chairs and Tables;
photo 1946 *by Charles Eames.*

Top left:
Square wood Coffee Table and LCM
Chair; photo 1950 *by Charles Eames.*

Top right:
Eames Molded Plywood Table; photo
1994 *by Phil Schaafsma.*

Right:
CTM (Round Coffee Table, metal) with
three metal legs; photo 1946 *by
Charles Eames.*

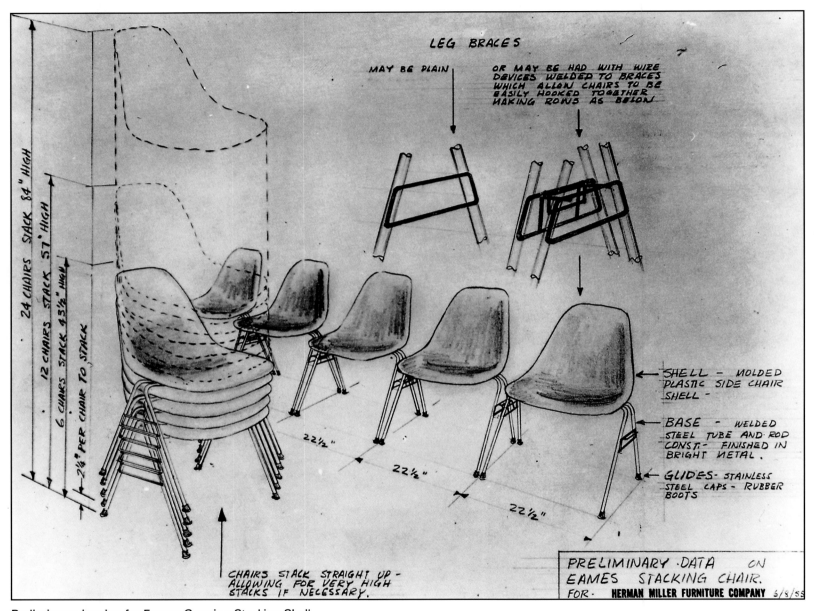

Preliminary drawing for Eames Ganging Stacking Shell
Chair, showing measurements and details, dated 6-8-55.

Stacked bases for Molded Plywood Chairs; *photo by Charles Eames.*

Molded Plastic Side Chair with Eiffel Tower Base.

35

Three black metal frames showing the progression of
the Eiffel Tower wire bases; *photo by Charles Eames.*

Group of unupholstered Wire Chairs with Eiffel Tower
bases, and a crow; photo 1952 *by Charles Eames.*

37

Composite photograph of nine images of Wire Chairs and Sofa Compact prototype; photo 1960 *by Charles Eames.*

Opposite:
Group of Wire Chairs in abstract pattern; photo 1951 *by Charles Eames.*

39

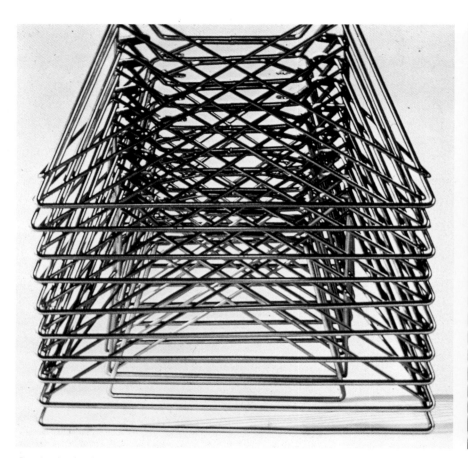

Stacked wire bases.

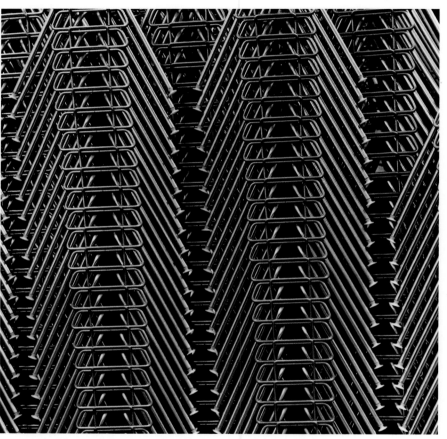

Ganging-Stacking Chair Bases; *photo by Charles Eames.*

Group of forty-four Molded
Fiberglass Chairs, including
upholstered Sideshells,
Armshells, and Wire Chairs
with various bases; photo
1965 *by West Dempster.*

Molded Fiberglass and Plywood Chairs, 127
Chairs, and Secretarial Chairs; photo 1972.

"La Chaise" or Chaise of fiberglass, iron rods, and wood; two thin fiberglass shells are glued together and separated by a hard rubber disc, and the resulting cavity is filled with styrene. Designed in 1948, it was not produced until 1990, by Vitra.

Detail.

Red Molded Fiber-
glass Ganging-
Stacking Chairs,
Educational Seating,
and Stools, photo
1973 *by Earl Woods.*

Split upholstery
Armshells with
Contract and Four-Leg
Bases, in various
colors; photo 1976.

Opposite:
Close up of group of red
Shell Chairs; photo 1973
by Earl Woods.

Blue upholstered
LaFonda Armshells
and Sideshells with
Standard Armshells
and Sideshells, on
LaFonda and
Contract Bases;
photo 1973 *by Earl
Woods.*

Examples of Eames
Universal Base with
Molded Fiberglass
Shells and Secretarial
Chairs, all with
casters, photo 1978
by Earl Woods.

4-Leg Base upholstered EC 127 Chairs around rectangular Conference
Table with 2-Leg Contract Base; photo 1970 *by Earl Woods.*

Eames 4-Leg Base spread with Side and
Armshells, Molded Plywood Chairs, and an
EC127 Chair¡ photo 1978 *by Earl Woods*.

Molded Plastic Shell Arm
Chair in Crimson, with wire
legs and birch rockers
(top); Wire Chair with Eiffel
Tower legs (left center);
Molded Plastic Side Chair
(right center) and LCM
Chair; photo 1960 *by
Rooks Studios.*

Sofa Compact prototype frame showing a wire mesh back truss support
and four wood feet, without cushions; *photo by Charles Eames.*

Front view of fabric upholstered Sofa Compact;
photo 1985 *by Bill Sharpe, J.D. Thomas.*

Front view of red fabric upholstered Sofa
Compact; photo 1972 *by Earl Woods.*

Black leather upholstered molded plywood 670/671
Lounge Chair and Ottoman; photo 1978 *by Earl Woods.*

The Lounge and Ottoman were originally built in 1956 as a birthday present for the Eameses' good friend, film director Billy Wilder. Although not intended for mass production, it has been produced continuously and copied widely. Originally of molded Brazilian rosewood, the endangered wood species is no longer used; it was replaced with walnut or cherry in 1990. Originally, the duck down cushions were available in several upholstery choices, but it has only been produced in leather since 1962, and the cushions have been urethane foam wrapped in polyester fiberfill since 1979. It won the Milan Triennale in 1957 and is in the permanent collection of the Museum of Modern Art.

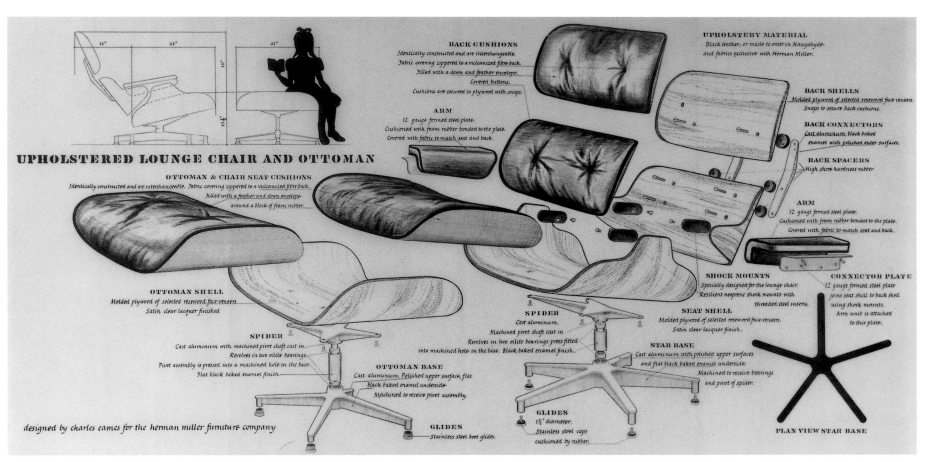

UPHOLSTERED LOUNGE CHAIR AND OTTOMAN

BACK CUSHIONS
Identically constructed and are interchangeable.
Fabric covering zippered to a vulcanized fibre back.
Filled with a down and feather envelope.
Covered buttons.
Cushions are secured to plywood with snaps.

UPHOLSTERY MATERIAL
Black leather, or made to order in Naugahyde
and fabrics exclusive with Herman Miller.

BACK SHELLS
Molded plywood of selected rosewood face veneers.
Snaps to secure back cushions.

BACK CONNECTORS
Cast aluminum, black baked
enamel with polished outer surfaces.

BACK SPACERS
High short-hardness rubber

ARM
12 gauge formed steel plate.
Cushioned with foam rubber bonded to the plate.
Covered with fabric to match seat and back.

ARM
12 gauge formed steel plate.
Cushioned with foam rubber bonded to the plate.
Covered with fabric to match seat and back.

OTTOMAN & CHAIR SEAT CUSHIONS
Identically constructed and are interchangeable. Fabric covering zippered to a vulcanized fibre back.
Filled with a feather and down envelope
around a block of foam rubber.

OTTOMAN SHELL
Molded plywood of selected rosewood face veneers.
Satin clear lacquer finished.

SHOCK MOUNTS
Specially designed for the lounge chair.
Resilient neoprene shock mounts with
threaded steel inserts.

CONNECTOR PLATE
12 gauge formed steel plate
joins seat shell to back shell
using shock mounts.
Arm unit is attached
to this plate.

SPIDER
Cast aluminum.
Machined pivot shaft cast in.
Revolves in two oilite bearings press fitted
into machined hole in the base. Black baked enamel finish.

SEAT SHELL
Molded plywood of selected rosewood face veneers.
Satin clear lacquer finish.

SPIDER
Cast aluminum with machined pivot shaft cast in.
Revolves in two oilite bearings.
Pivot assembly is pressed into a machined hole in the base.
Flat black baked enamel finish.

STAR BASE
Cast aluminum with polished upper surfaces
and flat black baked enamel underside.
Machined to receive bearings
and pivot of spider.

OTTOMAN BASE
Cast aluminum. Polished upper surface, flat
black baked enamel underside.
Machined to receive pivot assembly.

GLIDES
1½" diameter.
Stainless steel caps
cushioned by rubber.

PLAN VIEW STAR BASE

GLIDES
Stainless steel boot glides.

designed by charles eames for the herman miller furniture company

Exploded view of Eames Lounge and
Ottoman, drawing by Charles Kratka, 1958.

59

Stacks of molded plywood for Eames Lounges.

Above left:
Lounge being assembled.

Above right:
Norman Rockwell style pose of woman sitting in Aluminum Group Lounge and Ottoman and a man in the 570/671 Lounge and Ottoman; photo 1960.

Left:
Lounge pictured in Herman Miller brochure *Reference Points* in 1985.

Aluminum Management Chair with casters;
photo 1985 *by Bill Sharpe, J.D. Thomas.*

Aluminum Lounge and Ottoman; photo
1985 *by Bill Sharpe, J.D. Thomas.*

Opposite:
Close-up view of back
of Aluminum High
Back Chair.

Eames Aluminum Group Chairs; photo 1974 *by Earl Woods.*

Aluminum Lounge Chair without arms; photo 1972 *by Earl Woods.*

Three views of Eames (Time-Life) Executive Chair; photo 1973 *by Earl Woods.*

Although originally designed in 1960 for the lobby of the Time-Life Building in New York, this padded leather swivel chair is also known as the "Bobby Fischer," because he used it in the World Chess Championship in Reykjavik in 1972. When it was admired by his opponent, Boris Spassky, Herman Miller had one flown in for the Russian chess master as well.

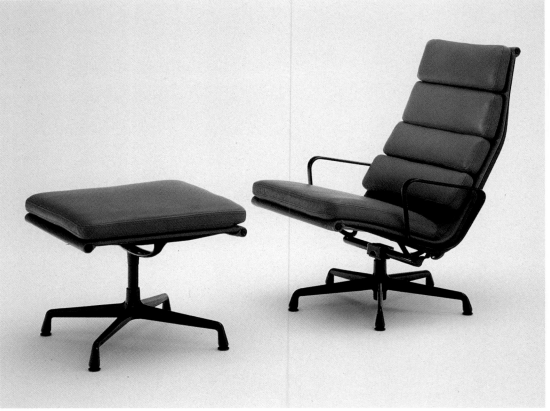

Left:
Soft Pad Management Chair with
black leather upholstery and 5-star
base; photo 1989 *by Earl Woods.*

Above:
Soft Pad Lounge and Ottoman from
1992 Catalog; *photo by William Sharpe.*

Nine-seat Tandem Sling Seating unit chained to a pickup truck
with a man reading a paper; photo 1965 *by Charles Eames.*

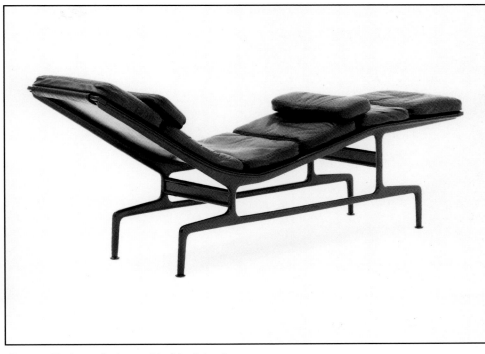

Eames Chaise upholstered in black leather,
made from 1968 on; photo 1980 *by Earl Woods.*

Tandem Sling Seating was originally designed for Chicago's O'Hare
Airport and installed in Chicago and the Dulles International Airport
in Washington, D.C. in 1962. Seat and back pads are of heat-sealed
vinyl and stretched between cast aluminum frames. Seats are
secured to a single, continuous, steel T-beam. Identical back and
seat pads were designed to be easily and inexpensively replaced.

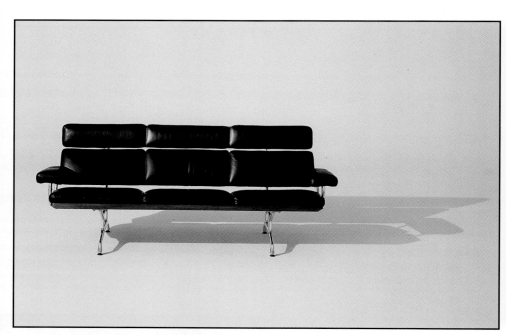

Soft Pad Sofa, also called 3-Seat Sofa, the last Eames
design, made from 1984 on; *photo by Phil Schaafsma.*

"The Most Original American
Furniture Designer Since
Duncan Phyfe"

That's what the late Charles Eames was called in a Museum of Modern Art catalog. This sofa, produced now for the first time, is the last product to be designed by Eames and his wife and design partner Ray. The frame is oiled teak or walnut, and cast aluminum with polished or espresso finish. The cushions are covered in black, brown, or espresso leather.

Fred Olsen's drawing of the sofa is from *Reference Points*, a book of furniture portraits by nine artists. Other pieces in the volume have been designed by Eames, George Nelson, and Isamu Noguchi, with colors and fabrics by Clino Castelli.

For a limited time, a copy of *Reference Points* will be included with an order for any of the pieces portrayed. For information about the furniture, or *Reference Points*, call 1 800 851 1196. Within Michigan call collect (616) 772 3442. Or, write Kathy Keating, *Reference Points*, Herman Miller, Inc., Zeeland, Michigan 49464.

herman miller

Promotional graphic of Soft Pad Sofa
from the brochure *Reference Points*.

Round Dining Table (Segmented Base Table), resembling La Fonda table, but with single column base, made from 1964 on; *photo Phil Schaafsma.*

Round LaFonda Table with a plastic top and double column base, designed for Alexander Girard's project, La Fonda del Sol restaurant, and produced from 1961 on; photo 1970.

Rectangular Dining Table (Segmented Base Table), 36" x 72", made from 1964 on; *photo Phil Schaafsma.*

69

Segmented Base Tables.

Elliptical Table (Surf-board Table), pro-duced 1951-1964 and reintroduced in 1994; *photo Phil Schaafsma.*

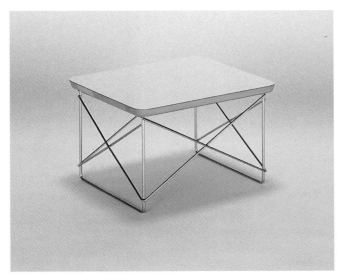

Wire Base Table (LTR), a low table with wire base, produced 1950 on; *photo Bill Lindhout.*

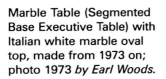

Marble Table (Segmented Base Executive Table) with Italian white marble oval top, made from 1973 on; photo 1973 *by Earl Woods.*

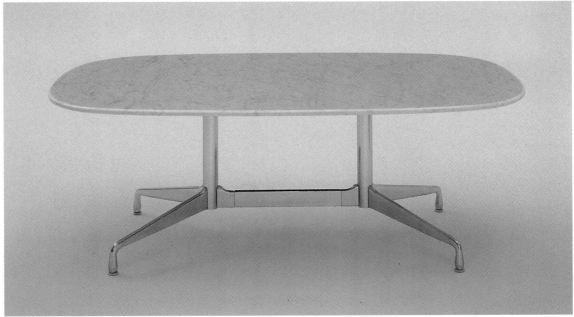

71

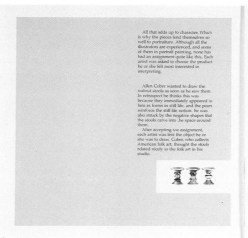

All that adds up to character. Which is why the pieces lend themselves so well to portraiture. Although all the illustrators are experienced, and some of them in portrait painting, none has had an assignment quite like this. Each artist was asked to choose the product he or she felt most interested in interpreting.

Allen Cober wanted to draw the walnut stools as soon as he saw them. In retrospect he thinks this was because they immediately appeared to him as forms in still life, and the pears reinforce the still life notion. he was also struck by the negative shapes that the stools carve into the space around them.

After accepting the assignment, each artist was lent the object he or she was to draw. Cober, who collects American folk art, thought the stools related nicely to the folk art in his studio.

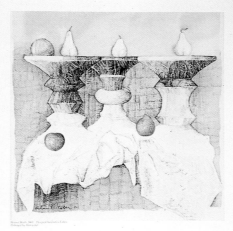

Above:
The three versions (411, 412, and 413) of the Walnut Stools, designed by Ray Eames for the Time-Life Building in 1960 and produced continuously, photo 1987 *by Earl Woods.*

Left:
Eames Stools illustrated in *Reference Points.*

Display showing varieties of Storage Units, produced
1950-1955; photo 1949 *by Charles Eames.*

Molded Plywood
Folding Screen (FSW),
produced 1946-1955
and reintroduced in
1994. *Photo Phil
Schaafsma.*

74

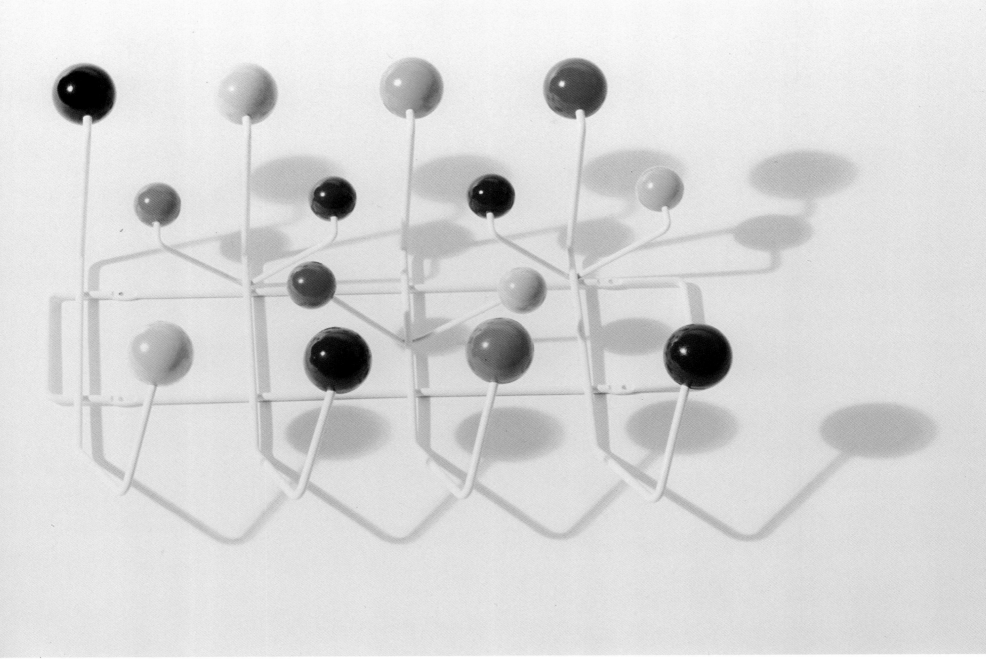

"Hang-It-All," the children's clothes hanger, produced from
1953 to 1961 and reintroduced in 1994; *photo Phil Schaafsma.*

Chapter 2

George Nelson

*"Total design as it appears to me is
nothing more or less than a process
of relating everything to everything."*

Nelson in a sports car with a dog, c. 1950.

Nelson, c. 1950.

George Nelson (1908-1986)

Architect, industrial designer, and author, George Nelson was one of the great designers of the twentieth century. He was born in Hartford, Connecticut in 1908. His father, Simeon, came to the United States from Russia at age fifteen and later became a pharmacist with his own drug store. His mother, Lilian Canterow Nelson, was born in the United States; both of her parents were physicians. In 1924, at the age of sixteen, Nelson entered Yale University to study architecture. He graduated in 1928 with a Bachelor of Arts degree and then earned a Bachelor of Fine Arts degree from Yale in 1931, followed by graduate work at Catholic University in Washington, D.C. From 1932 to 1934 he attended graduate school on fellowship at the American Academy in Rome and was awarded the Prix de Rome for architecture. More interested in writing about architecture than in practicing it, when he returned to the United States he joined the staff of *Architectural Forum* as associate editor from 1935-1943, and then became co-managing editor until 1944. During those same years, he developed his career as an industrial designer, became a registered architect in the state of New York, and joined the faculty at Yale.

Gilbert Rohde was the first to introduce modern design to Herman Miller, but when he died suddenly at age 49 in 1944, the company was left without design direction. Herman Miller founder Dirk Jan (D.J.) De Pree became interested in Nelson after reading an article he had written for *Architectural Forum* about a storage wall he and Henry Wright had designed. Although Nelson insisted that he was not a furniture designer and knew nothing about the furniture industry, he became the first Director of Design at Herman Miller in 1946. He remained until 1972, then continued as a consultant designer until he died in 1986. While designing for Herman Miller, Nelson also ran his own design firm, George Nelson & Co. (and variations of the name) which he formed in 1947. In 1953,

with Gordon Chadwick, former Wright apprentice, he formed an architectural partnership. His first marriage to Frances Hollister, in 1933, ended in divorce, and in 1960 he married Jacqueline Wilkenson; he had three sons, Hollister, Peter, and Mico.

The list of Nelson's accomplishments (*see Abercrombie*) is astounding. They range from publications on design and design philosophy, to furniture that would help form the definition of modernism. His first Herman Miller collection in 1946, totaling about eighty pieces, was a collaboration with Irving Harper and Ernest Farmer. In addition to furniture, Nelson designed the 1949 collection of modern clocks and the Bubble Lamps for the Howard Miller Clock Co., Herman Miller showrooms, catalogs, graphics, textiles, dinnerware, glassware, and interiors. He designed the Chrysler Exhibit and co-designed the Irish Pavilion at the New York World's Fair and he was in charge of the design and execution of the United States Exhibit in Moscow in 1959. As editor of *Architectural Forum,* he helped it become a major critical force. He also wrote numerous thought-provoking books and articles on design and his observations of the world. Awards include Best Office of the Year from the *New York Times* in 1953; Gold Medal, Art Directors Club of New York in 1953; Good Design award, Museum of Modern Art in 1954; Product Design Award, Milan Triennale; 1954 Trailblazer Award for Furniture Design, National Home Furnishings League; and numerous others for design excellence.

Ettore Sottsass Jr. presented a subjective, yet unmatched, description of Nelson in the foreword of Stanley Abercrombie's biography. On a winter night in Milan, Nelson had visited Sottsass, who later wrote:

> I don't know if you have ever happened to receive a calm, absolutely calm man in your house, and suddenly to know that the air around you has changed, that words have changed, that all the normal reference points of your life have

changed — to realize all of a sudden that you've got to speed up the whole general method, speed up your visions, your programs, or maybe even your entire utopia.

Nelson had a clear philosophy of design, which he condensed into five principles: 1) what you make is important; 2) design is an integral part of the business; 3) the product must be honest; 4) you decide what you want to make; and 5) there is a market for good design. He said, "...it seems ridiculously easy to help a business grow to its full potential — if certain crucial factors are present. The most important is a manufacturer with sufficient vision to see beyond the end of its nose, a quality not nearly so common as it might be."

George Nelson became well known for his views and for his ability to present them eloquently. The world according to Nelson is always one worth reading about, and his article for the January 1947 issue of *Fortune* magazine entitled "The Furniture Industry" can be included in any analysis of postwar American furniture, taste, or culture. It also helps to explain the widespread resistance to modernism and the magnitude of risk and pioneering spirit found at Herman Miller in 1946.

At the time Nelson joined Herman Miller the American furniture industry was the second largest producer of consumer durable goods in the country. There were furniture manufacturing facilities in nearly every state, and many of the 3,500 manufacturers were operating out of garages and basements. The economic outlook was excellent in spite of the products being "endlessly and unnecessarily varied, and almost uniformly uninspired."

One explanation for the lack of inspiration, Nelson observed, was that most factories were equipped to work only in the single traditional material, wood. Since wood construction can be performed in small shops as easily as in large factories, there were many small shops scattered about in small towns. As a result, most manufacturers lacked the capital for research and the opportunity it gave to move beyond craft status. To further minimize any incentive for change, "the more typical manufacturer can sell almost anything he can squeeze out of his antiquated plant." Nelson quotes an unidentified furniture buyer who remarked, "You could blow up 2,900 out of 3,000 furniture plants and not damage the industry as far as constructive thinking and activity are concerned." (On the brighter side, there could have been as many as 100 manufacturers who were at least attempting to think creatively.)

"Borax" was a term frequently used for cheap furniture that relied on extravagant styling to create a superficial effect of high cost — furniture of the lowest possible taste and quality. The most widely produced and purchased furniture types in the 1940s were the same as in preceding decades — either borax or period adaptations referred to as "traditional." And this traditional furniture ranged from well-crafted reproductions of well-designed period pieces, to thoughtless adaptations, referred to as "Grand Rapids Chippendale," to borax. In any case, the centuries preferred by furniture buyers in 1947 were the seventeenth and eighteenth, and Nelson observed that "the deeply rooted insistence on century-old prototypes in the industry...has been a major element on prolonging an already impressive technological lag."

A typical picture of the American furniture industry was of countless small furniture stores selling cheap generic furniture made by either a small shop or a big company. And "the place to see the industry run — in all directions at once — is at the furniture market, a merchandising device with half the charm and twice the efficiency of the medieval fair at ancient Novogorod.... Ninety-eight percent of the furniture on display is appalling in its colorless mediocrity, and half of it is so outrageously bad that one no longer wonders why the average American home is as tastelessly furnished as any in the world." A significant portion of the remaining two percent — the colorful and outstanding that Nelson alluded to — was presumably found in the Herman Miller showrooms, such as the one in the Chicago Merchandise Mart.

Nelson designed many of these showrooms as well as their contents. He was responsible for giving direction to Herman Miller by designing or bringing designers aboard who brought us the classics. Hugh De Pree writes, "There is no doubt that George Nelson was the most creative designer in our lives...George was not only a designer at Herman Miller, but also a leader, a consultant, a resource, a teacher. He contributed so much but was recognized so inadequately. We who knew him would never be the same" (47)....and "He saw design as a larger consideration than product design. He saw the need for designing the company" (43).

As Abercrombie observed, "The idea of paraphrasing Nelson's prose seems ridiculous." The following glimpses into Nelson's philosophy (about design and just about everything else) are from the book *George Nelson on Design:*

There is no such thing as a creative profession. There are as many hacks in architecture, graphics and industrial design as there are in banking, garbage collection or any faculty in any university. *Only individuals can be creative.* (21)

We cannot *think* our way into creative behavior. (20)

What the creative act really means is the unfolding of the human psyche in the sudden realization that one has taken a lot of disconnected pieces and *found,* not *done* a way of putting them together. This is when the solitary individual finds he is connected with a reality he never dreamed of, with a feeling of internal power without limit, and the knowledge that he is truly and fully

Nelson, c. 1989; *photo Melissa Brown.*

alive for one miraculous instant....Peaks are of very short duration, possibly because none of us could live through a longer exposure. (21-22)

From a 1965 interview with *Interiors* magazine:

On affluence:
The current consumer orgies should give most self-respecting industrial designers a belly-ache. It also means a designer can get rich enough so he can quit work and ride around in the fiber glass boat he designed the year before.

79

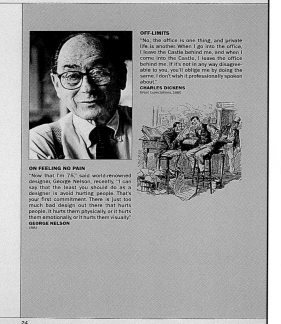

The boxed insert contains:

private rooms with tables (for confidential discussions). Groups also need the motivation to communicate (something the environment can only help to engender).

Groups need some sort of identification—some place they can call their own, some way to distinguish themselves. Groups need leadership. Like most sanctuaries and the House of Representatives, office environments establish leadership—and the style of leadership—by the simple positioning of a person. Groups inevitably have conflicts, constructive ones, we hope. Though an environment will never guarantee the drive to participate toward a common goal, it can provide an atmosphere where conflict can be mediated and resolved. It can bring together or it can separate. It can foster an old attitude spoken of by Max De Pree, the "freedom to fail," or it can inhibit the expression of opinion and idea.

A lot of work these days is office work. We say groups are drawn together to do office work, but as we scan the working world today, we see that more and more of what's being done, even when it doesn't take place in an office, looks like office work. Laboratory work looks like office work. Indeed, a recent British study has found that workers in labs spend only thirteen percent of their time operating equipment. By contrast, a "scientist's day" consists largely of "talking face to face" (35%), "reading" (12%), "writing" (12%), and "talking by telephone" (7%).

Even production lines for computer boards call for office-like procedures: technicians stationed in clean and discrete "offices," surrounded by small piles of chips ready to be assembled, perhaps with the aid of a robot—not unlike production workers who process claims at Blue Cross.

ON FEELING NO PAIN
"Now that I'm 75," said world-renowned designer, George Nelson, recently, "I can say that the least you should do as a designer is avoid hurting people. That's your first commitment. There is just too much bad design out there that hurts people. It hurts them physically, or it hurts them emotionally, or it hurts them visually."
GEORGE NELSON
1984

OFF-LIMITS
"No; the office is one thing, and private life is another. When I go into the office, I leave the Castle behind me, and when I come into the Castle, I leave the office behind me. If it's not in any way disagreeable to you, you'll oblige me by doing the same. I don't wish it professionally spoken about."
CHARLES DICKENS
Great Expectations, 1860

24

"...the least you should do as a designer is avoid hurting people....There is just too much bad design out there that hurts people. It hurts them physically, or it hurts them emotionally, or it hurts them visually."(from *Everybodys Business* by the Herman Miller Research Corporation, 1984)

The trouble here in our office is that we haven't designed any fiber glass boats.

Pioneer Americans moving into this continent make me think of a [primitive] tribe moving into a deserted Versailles. They mess up the first apartment with their garbage and excrement, then move onto the second apartment. Then the third and the fourth, until they come to the end of the place. Then some guy has an absolute brain wave: Why not go back and clean up the muck in the first apartment?...And that's just about where we are in the U.S. today. (138)

In 1984 Herman Miller provided a generous grant to the University of Michigan to create a visiting professorship. This enabled Nelson to be Professor of Design Research until he died two years later. The University then published a booklet by Nelson entitled "Changing the World." The following excerpts are from this posthumous publication:

...design, whether in the form of buildings or articles of use and consumption, does not change the world: it *reflects* changes already going on, which is a very different story.

On the Serengeti plains in Africa, millions of animals graze, moving slowly from one area to another. Among these animals there are perhaps fifty thousand predators which live off them. The animals graze, apparently oblivious to everything but the next clump of grass. Then a single predator is sensed, a wave of tension runs through the group, and they take off in panic. People do the same thing. They graze peacefully on corporate files or whatever fodder is lying around, bothering no one. Then something unfamiliar shows up, often an idea, and they become alert.

Mass societies have a way of picking the most mediocre leaders whenever they are given the opportunity.

...personal freedom is being steadily eroded and the rugged individual who used to be the American model is finding fewer and fewer places where it is comfortable for him to be either rugged or an individual.

You get a kind of educational bureaucracy philosophy which operates in public institutions, that a kid is a deflated tire and, if you pump him up to sixty pounds, he's educated.

All healthy children seem to display some of the qualities of the creative individual....this vital quality they exhibit is beaten out of them by parents or teachers, or squeezed out, by the time they reach adolescence. And by the time they are adults, they are as dull, uninteresting, and mentally lazy as their elders. This is how they are trained to 'fit in'....a minute percentage of the victims who escape this fate...I have come to suspect, is the rare minority which changes the world.

All brainstorming does is get a lot of people together to talk without listening to each other.

Learning is what happens when you open a dictionary to find out how to spell a word or what it really means, and you find yourself wasting an hour reading the dictionary because it's so fascinating to see all these funny words on that page, most of which you've never seen before.

Nelson's serious regard for the environment and the human condition permeate all of his writing, and his insight and wit, and even his cynicism, keep the reader in touch with the issues. Although Nelson usually wrote about design, he never restricted himself to just objects. Design is not about things, it is about problems and solutions, and Nelson pointed to the universal even when he was discussing a specific problem. He was in good company with personalities like Girard, the Eameses, and with the leadership at Herman Miller. Without their common values, acute awareness of responsibility, vision, and perfect timing, neither the company nor its superstar designers could have pulled it off. Hugh De Pree called it providential. Perhaps it was.

Nelson, c. 1981.

Group of Nelson Bubble Lamps made by Howard Miller Clock Co; photo 1960.

Nelson products for Herman Miller

Action Office I,1964-1970. Concept by Bob Propst

Basic Cabinet Series, 1946-1958. Basic cabinets differed from Steelframe Case Group in that doors or drawers were set into paneled, box-like frames that concealed its functional equipment behind hinged or sliding doors. Basic Cabinets differed from Thin Edge cases in the hardware used to open the doors and in the frame itself — the Basic Cabinet frame was wider, about 3/4-inch, as opposed to the 3/8-inch of Thin Edge cases.

Basic Storage Components, 1949-1954. Built-in storage system installed by a contractor.

Beds, 1946-1964. Daybed introduced 1950; Convertible Sleeping Sofa introduced 1956; Thin Edge Bed introduced 1956.

Black Frame Group, 1961-1963. Often confused with 9000 Series Executive Office Group and the Cube Group, but Black Frame is strictly residential and has no executive desks. The Black Frame Slat Bench was often confused with the Platform Bench. However, the Black Frame had four legs that were flush with the top slats, while the Platform had inset trapezoid-shaped legs.

Catenary Group, 1963-1968. Metal upholstered Lounge seat, Ottoman, and Coffee Table with all metallic joints chemically bonded, providing extra strength and allowing parts to be plated and polished before assembly.

Chaise, 1956-?.

Coconut Chair, 1955-1978. An Ottoman was designed in 1958.

Comprehensive Storage System, 1959-1973.

Comprehensive Panel System, 1967-1973.

Contract Benches, 1959-1970.

Cube Group, 1967-1974. Seating, coffee tables, desks, and storage units.

Executive Office Group, 1952-1978. The EOG with its L-shaped desk was originally designed by Rohde and his staff in 1939; after Rohde died, one of his designers, Ernest Farmer joined the Nelson office when Nelson became design director of Herman Miller.

Executive Office Group 9000 Series, 1956-c.1963.

Flying Duck Chair, 1955 only.

Gate Leg Tables, 1946-1960.

Kangaroo Chair, 1956-1964.

Library Group, 1965-1975. Designed by Nelson, Propst and the Herman Miller Product Development Group.

Light Office Chairs, 1971-1978.

Loose Cushion Group, 1956-?.

Marshmallow Sofa, 1956-1965. Designed by Irving Harper of George Nelson Associates, made with 22 interchangeable discs attached to the metal frame; only 186 were produced between 1957 and 1961.

Miniature Cases, 1954-c.1963; reissued 1994. Small teak cabinets with white pulls originally designed to go with Rosewood cases.

Modern Management Group, 1957-c.1962: Metal office furniture resembling the wood EOG design of 1963, except that the pulls were squarish and placed in the center of the drawer face.

Modular Seating, 1956-1978. This was sometimes confused with Contract Benches and Steel Frame seating, but the Modular cushions had a strip of piping sewn around the cushion, giving it the appearance of double height, and the cushions had buttons sewn in a line across the back. Contract benches had no seat cushions with backs, and Steelframe seating cushions had no buttons.

Office Residential Desks, 1946-c.1957.

Pedestal Tables, 1954-present.

Platform Benches, 1946-1967; reissued 1994. Originally called a Slat Bench, it became the Platform Bench when the Black Frame Group was introduced in 1961. The widths in 1946 were 48, 68, 72, and 102 inches. 56-3/16 and 92-inch widths were added in 1949. The reissued benches are available in 48 and 60-inch widths.

Pretzel Chairs, 1958 only. With or without circular seat cushions. ICF began to manufacture the chair in 1989, while Norman C. Cherner and Paul Goldman produced a similar chair called the Rockwell Chair for Plycraft.

Rosewood Group, 1952-1957. Similar to Thin Edge, but Rosewood cases had round pulls, 7-inch-long tapered legs, and rosewood stain. Earlier pieces had either black or white porcelain pulls, but by 1957 pulls were black or white plastic.

Sectional Seating, 1946-?.

Sling Loveseat, 1966-1968.

Sling Sofas, 1964 to present.

Steelframe Cases, 1954-?.

Steelframe Seating, 1954-1974.

Swaged Leg Group, 1958-1964. Chairs used molded plastic forms and shock-mounted connectors originally developed by Eames, but its flexibility made them different.

Thin Edge Cases, c. 1956 or 1958-?. Derived from the Rosewood Group, and often used the same hardware, making them easy to confuse.

End Table with Lamp and Planter, 1947-1956.

Executive Office Group: Secretarial "L" Desk with Penda Flex Basket, screen, and lamp all attached
to the table top, storage unit with shelf and two drawers, with yellow Side Shell Chair; photo 1955.

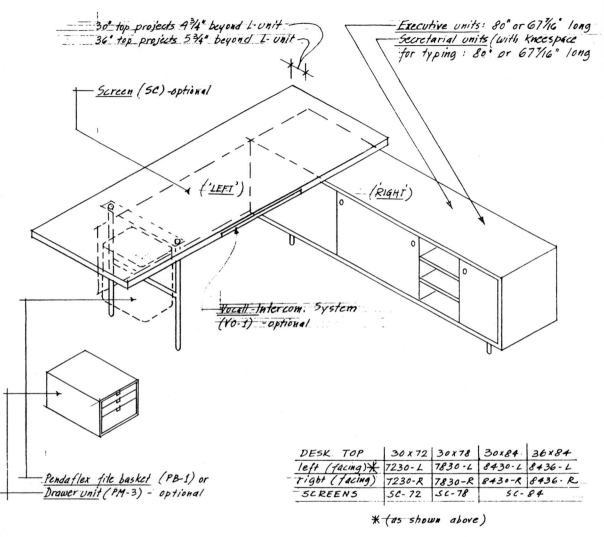

- 30" top projects 4¾" beyond L-unit
- 36" top projects 5¾" beyond L-unit

- Executive units: 80" or 67⁷⁄₁₆" long
- Secretarial units (with kneespace for typing: 80" or 67⁷⁄₁₆" long

- Screen (SC) -optional

('LEFT')

('RIGHT')

- Vocall-Intercom. System (VO-1) -optional

- Pendaflex file basket (PB-1) or
- Drawer unit (PM-3) - optional

DESK TOP	30 x 72	30 x 78	30 x 84	36 x 84
left (facing) ✳	7230-L	7830-L	8430-L	8436-L
right (facing)	7230-R	7830-R	8430-R	8436-R
SCREENS	SC-72	SC-78	SC-84	

✳ (as shown above)

add the following numbers for finishes of desk top:

Formica : 11 (add color). Formica Realwood - Prima Vera :12.
Formica Realwood - Walnut : 13. Linoleum : 16 (add color.)
Plastic fabric : 18 (add no. of fabric)

GEORGE NELSON

Above:
Executive Office Group: wooden single pedestal desk with two drawers and inset pulls and a wooden screen; photo 1971 *by Earl Woods.*

Left:
Drawing for the Executive Office Group (E.O.G.), dated 8-22-46

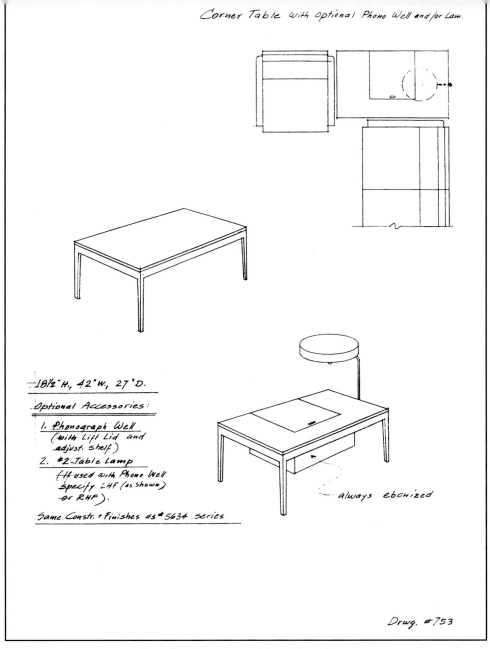

Corner Table with optional Phono. Well and/or Lam.

18½" H., 42"W, 27"D.

Optional Accessories:

1. Phonograph Well
   (with Lift Lid and
   adjust. shelf)
2. #2 Table Lamp
   (If used with Phono Well
   specify LHF (as shown)
   or RHF).

Same Constr. + Finishes as #5634 series

— always ebonized

Drwg. #753

Drawing for corner table with options.

Nelson Corner Table with attached lamp and planter; photo 1951.

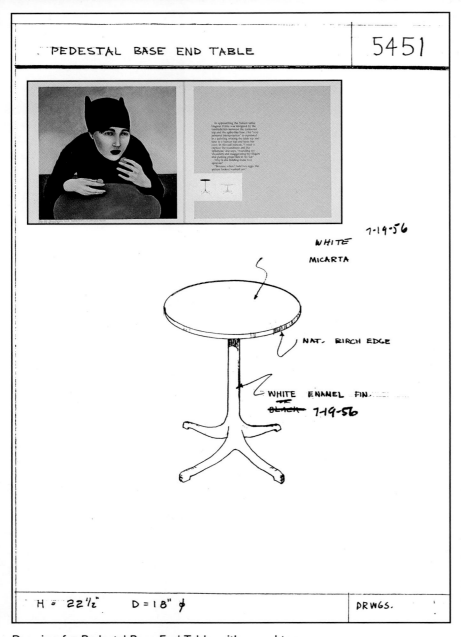

PEDESTAL BASE END TABLE   5451

WHITE   7·19·56
MICARTA

NAT. BIRCH EDGE

WHITE ENAMEL FIN.
BLACK 7·19·56

H = 22½"   D = 18" ⌀   DRWGS.

Drawing for Pedestal Base End Table with round top.

Inset:
Nelson End Table in *Reference Points*.

Nelson End Table (1954 —): gracefully sculpted pedestal and base, available in polished aluminum or white enamel; maple veneer edge on black or white laminate top in 17" or 28 1/2" diameter; photo 1978 *by Earl Woods*.

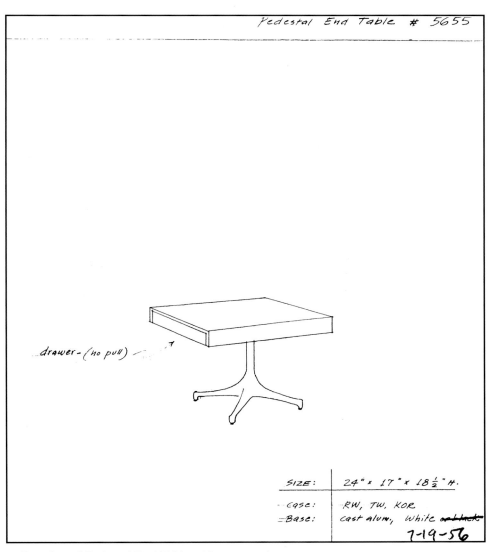

drawer - (no pull)

SIZE:	24" x 17" x 18½" H.
Case:	RW, TW, KOR
Base:	Cast alum, White ~~or black~~
	7-19-56

Drawing of Pedestal End Table with rectangular top.

Nelson Pedestal End Table with rectangular top, single drawer without pull, and white enamel pedestal; photo 1956 *by Rooks Photography.*

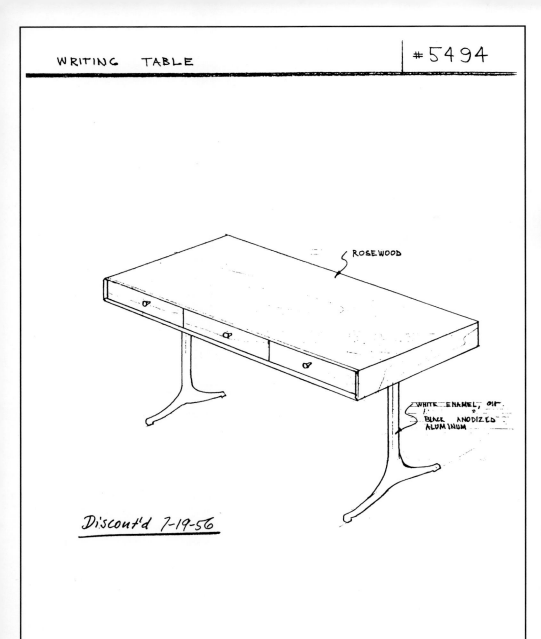

ROSEWOOD

WHITE ENAMEL, OIT
&
BLACK ANODIZED
ALUMINUM

Discont'd 7-19-56

W = 24"   H = 28½"   L = 42"

DRWG. 295
      316
      317
      338

Above:
Nelson Writing Table.

Left:
Drawing for Writing Table with
anodized aluminum base.

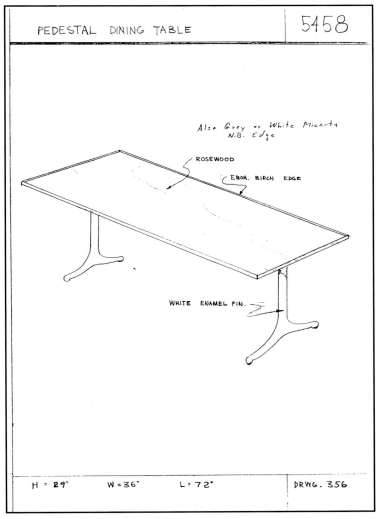

PEDESTAL DINING TABLE | 5458

Also Grey or White Micarta
N.B. Edge

ROSEWOOD

EBON. BIRCH EDGE

WHITE ENAMEL FIN.

| H = 29" | W = 36" | L = 72" | DRWG. 356 |

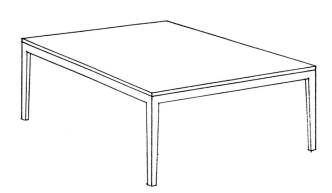

SIZE:	32" x 32" x 15" H.
TOP:	~~TW, KOR, white Mic, RW~~ W, OW, T, OT, OR, M-1
BASE:	~~TW, KOR, Ebonized (with RW top)~~ W, OW, T, OT, EB

see Detail Drwg # 461-B

Above left:
Drawing for Pedestal Dining Table.

Above right:
Drawing for Square Coffee & Corner
Table

Right:
Nelson square wood-grained Coffee
Table with ebonized legs; photo
1957 *by Rooks Photography.*

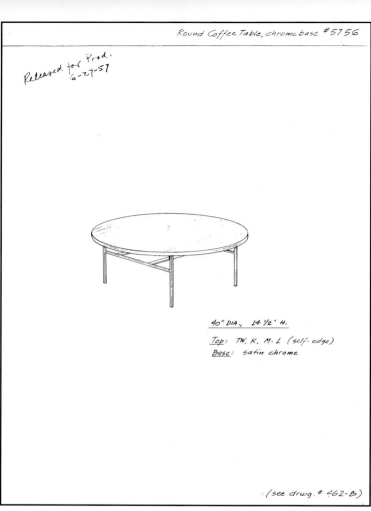

Round Coffee Table, chrome base #5756

Released for Prod.
6-27-57

40" DIA., 14 1/2" H.

Top: TW. K, M-L (self-edge)
Base: satin chrome

(see drwg. # 462-B)

Left:
Drawing for Round Coffee
Table with chrome base.

Right:
Nelson Round Coffee
Table on rectangular
chromed base with
crossbeams; photo 1960
by Rooks Photography.

90

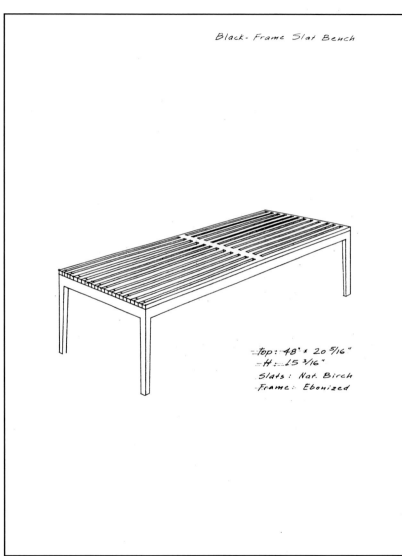

Black-Frame Slat Bench

Top: 48" x 20 5/16"
H: 15 3/16"
Slats: Nat. Birch
Frame: Ebonized

Nelson H-Leg Table, introduced in 1955; a wood grain conference table with legs in an H configuration like that used on some EOG desks; photo c. 1969.

Drawing for Black Frame Slat Bench, produced 1961-1963.

92

Nelson Platform Bench (1946-1967); one of the classics from Nelson's first collection and the 1948 catalog, solid maple with ebonized wood base; reintroduced in 1994 in Herman Miller for the Home in 48" and 60" lengths; *photo Phil Schaafsma.*

Nelson Basic Cabinet Series: bookcase cabinet with a hinged door beside an open area with a shelf, a television cabinet, radio, phonograph speaker cabinet with record storage, all on two Platform Benches; photo 1950 *by Dale Rooks.*

Nelson Basic Cabinet Series: chest cabinet with a full length door beside five drawers, drop front desk above three doors, radio, phonograph speaker cabinet, on metal arch legs, and a wood and upholstered chair; photo 1951 *by Dale Rooks.*

93

Nelson Basic Cabinet Series: Hotel Desk and vanity unit on a Platform
Bench with a low metal upholstered vanity seat; photo 1949.

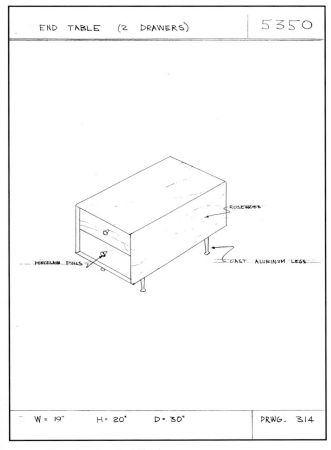

Drawing for End Table.

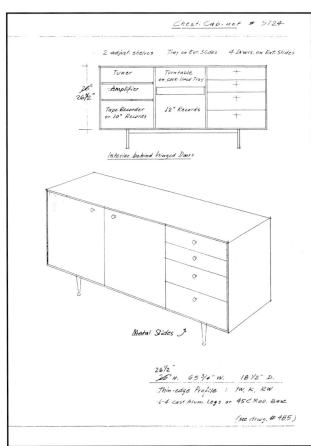

Drawing for Chest Cabinet

Three Nelson Miniature Cases stacked with doors or drawers open, bottom case on a pedestal; photo 1954.

Nelson Miniature Case (1954-1963): solid teak with rosewood stain on drawer fronts, white powder coated steel drawer pulls, dividers in middle drawer, white high pressure laminate top, turned brass feet, 14" x 30" x 5-5/8", reintroduced in 1994 in Herman Miller for the Home, discontinued 1997; *photo Phil Schaafsma.*

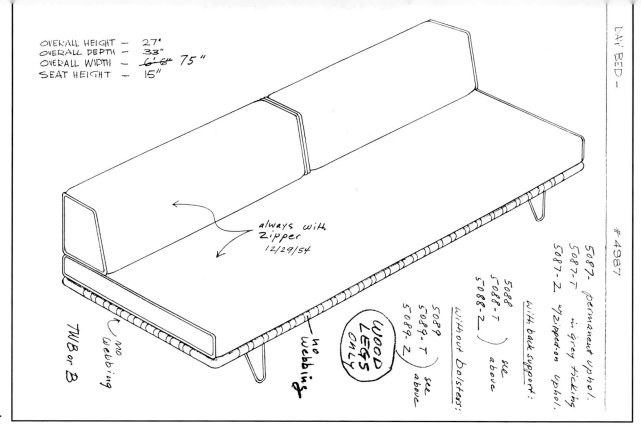

OVERALL HEIGHT – 27"
OVERALL DEPTH – 33"
OVERALL WIDTH – ~~6'8"~~ 75"
SEAT HEIGHT – 15"

4987

always with
Zipper
12/29/54

5087 – permanent uphol.
5087-T in grey ticking
5087-Z w/zipped-on uphol.

with back support:
5088
5088-T } see
5088-Z } above

without bolsters:
5089
5089-T } see
5089-Z } above

WOOD LEGS ONLY

no webbing

TWB or B

Drawing for Day Bed.

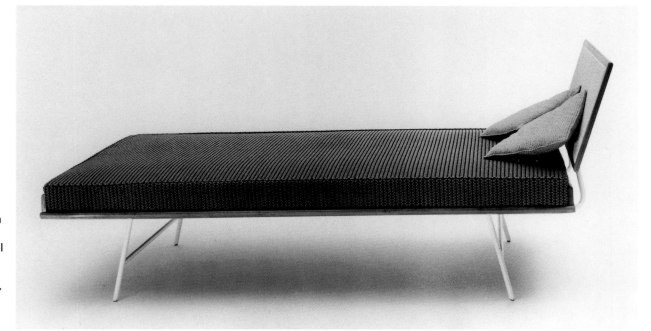

Nelson Thin Edge Bed with rectangular mattress on a wood slab with white metal tube legs, cane headboard and wood footboard, and two pillows; photo 1958 *by Rooks Photography.*

97

98

Nelson Daybed with rectangular mattress and two trapezoid back
cushions with a corner table and a László Coffee Table; photo 1949.

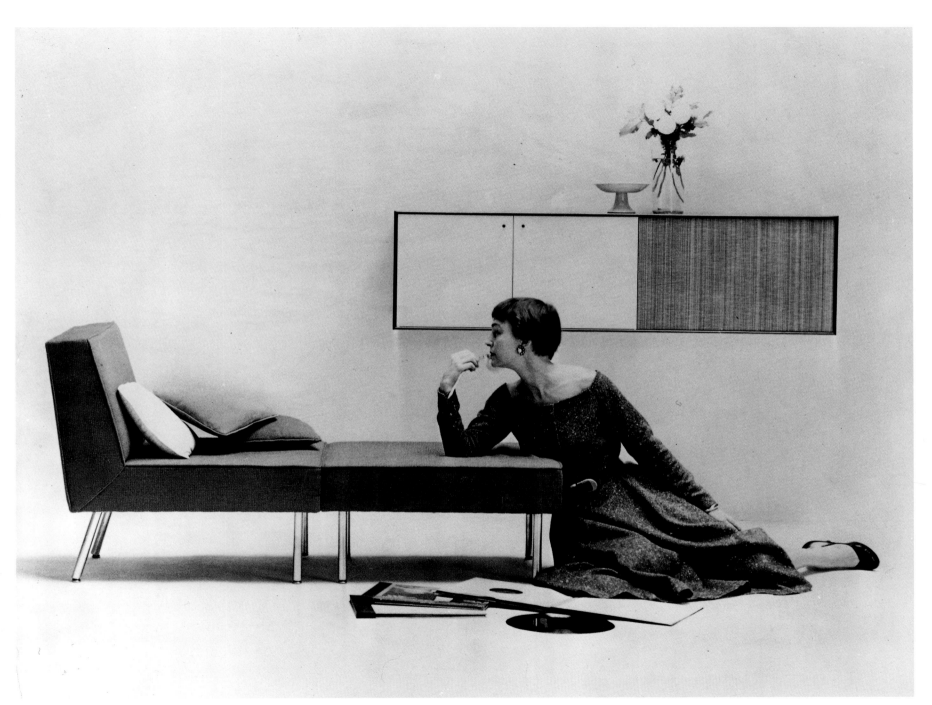

Wall mounted Thin Edge phonograph case,
with sectional chair and ottoman; photo 1958.

CHAISE

36" W x 26" H x 67" L

DRWG. 323 & 324

PBL. CHROME FRAME

5490

Left:
Drawing for Chaise.

Below:
Nelson Chaise, introduced
in 1956; photo 1956.

100

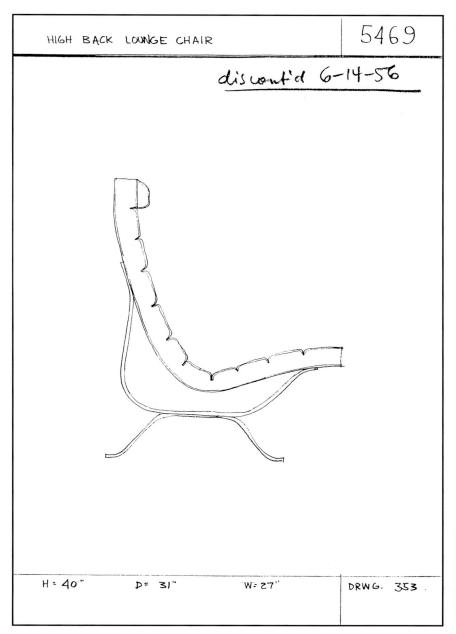

HIGH BACK LOUNGE CHAIR | 5469

discont'd 6-14-56

H = 40"   D = 31"   W = 27"   DRWG. 353

Drawing for High Back Lounge Chair.

Nelson High Back Lounge Chair with head rest
pillow and metal frame; photo 1954 *by Dale Rooks*.

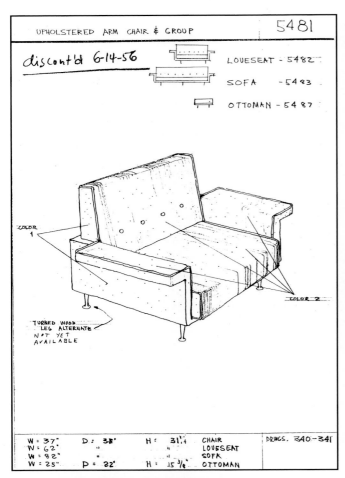

Drawing for Upholstered Arm Chair and group; the flared arms probably influenced Girard's chair designs about ten years later.

Nelson Love Seat with armrests flaring out like wings, with buttons, large seat cushion, on metal legs; photo 1954.

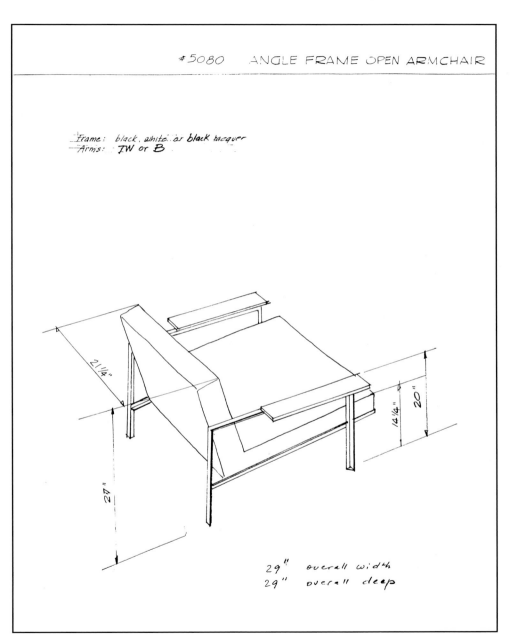

#5080   ANGLE FRAME OPEN ARMCHAIR

Frame: black, white or black lacquer
Arms: JW or B

21 1/4"

14 1/4"   20"

27"

29" overall width
29" overall deep

Drawing for Angle Frame open arm chair.

Angel Frame open armchair with metal frame, wood armrests, and upholstered seat back and cushions; photo 1958 *by Rooks Photography.*

Drawing for Knock-Down Chair.

Nelson Steelframe Knock-Down Chair with two striped cushions, possibly a prototype or special application; photo 1954.

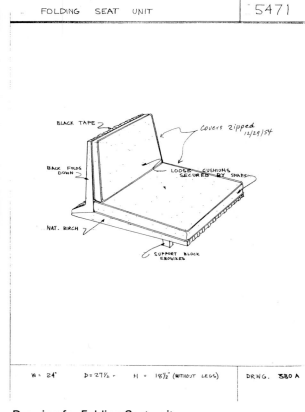

Drawing for Folding Seat unit.

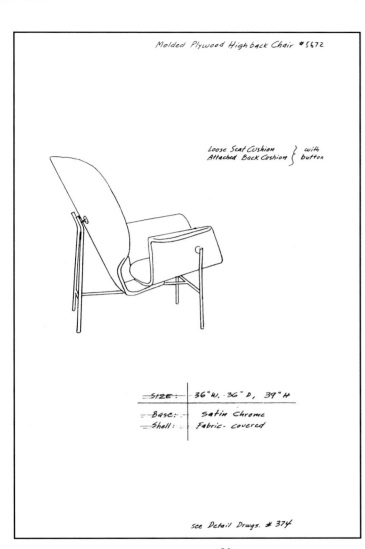

Molded Plywood Highback Chair #5672

Loose Seat Cushion } with
Attached Back Cushion } button

SIZE: 36"W, 36"D, 39"H

Base: Satin Chrome

Shell: Fabric-covered

see Detail Drwgs. # 374

Above:
Drawing for Molded
Plywood Highback Chair.

Right:
Nelson Kangaroo Chair:
upholstered chair with
closed curved arms, a
large cushioned back and
separate seat cushion on
a metal four-leg base;
photo 1958 *by Rooks
Photography.*

Nelson Pretzel Chair: These were residential chairs made of bentwood and available with or without circular seat cushions. The dining chair's most distinguishing feature was a large curved strip of bent birch plywood forming the back and arms. An armless version was also available with a short, curved plywood strip across the back bars. Properly called a "laminated wood chair," it was designed in 1958 in the Nelson Office by John Pile and others, according to Jacqueline Nelson. It was produced for only one year; photo 1958 *by Rooks Photography.*

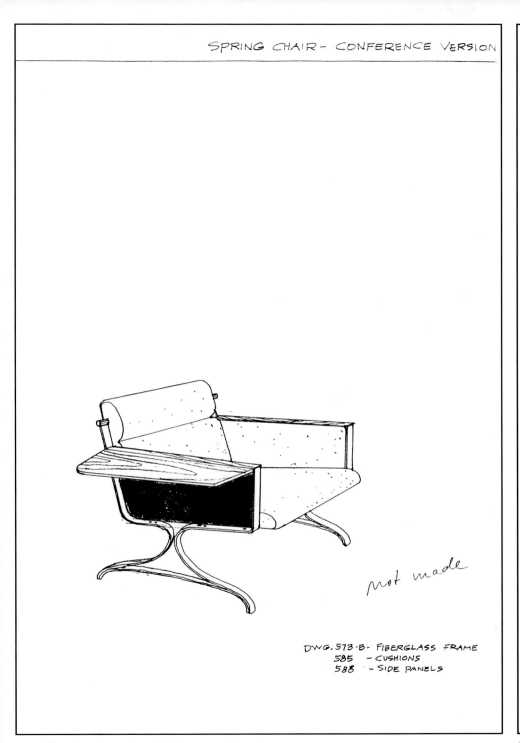

not made

DWG. 573-B- FIBERGLASS FRAME
585 — CUSHIONS
588 — SIDE PANELS

Drawing for spring chair, not produced.

ALSO WITH UPHOLSTERED ARM

not made

DRWGS. 573B - 585

Drawing for armless version of spring chair, not produced.

Nelson Coconut Chair
(1955-1978, produced
by Vitra since 1988);
wedge shaped chair
with curved edges and a
chromed base, its shell
is a molded plastic
semi-cone with form-
fitting foam cushions
and covered in bright
fabric, especially
polyknit, hopsak,
naugahyde, nylomix,
millerwood, milfrieze,
superwool or leather. In
1958 a matching
ottoman was produced
in a somewhat oval
form resting on four
legs; photo 1971 *by Earl
Woods.*

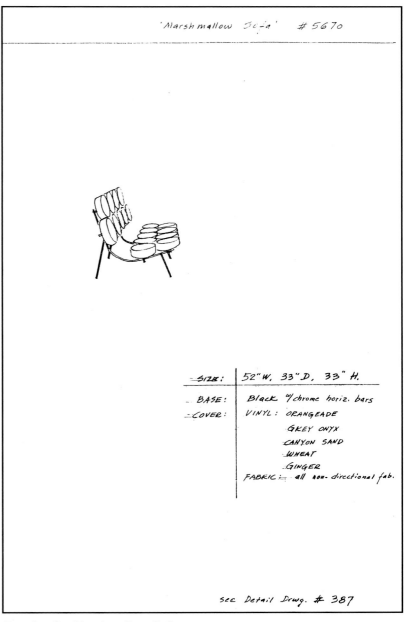

'Marshmallow Sofa' #5670

SIZE: 52"W, 33"D, 33"H.
BASE: Black w/chrome horiz. bars
COVER: VINYL: ORANGEADE
GREY ONYX
CANYON SAND
WHEAT
GINGER
FABRIC: all non-directional fab.

see Detail Drwg. # 387

Nelson Flying Duck Chair (1955): metal and upholstered office chair with curved, closed arms and a separate back cushion on a thin four-point metal base with casters resembling the Eames Contract Base, probably a prototype according to Jackie Nelson (5/19/89). It listed for $348 ($400 in leather) in the 1955/56 catalog; photo 1957 *by Rooks Photography.*

Drawing for Marshmallow Sofa.

Nelson Marshmallow Sofa with black metal frame and eighteen round "marshmallow" cushions with fabric upholstery. Designed for both residential and non-residential use, this sofa gained notoriety for its playful appearance. Between 1957 and 1961 there were only 186 produced; photo 1956 *by Rooks Photography.*

Woman sitting on Marshmallow Sofa showing construction
of back; photo 1956 *by Lionel Freedman.*

Man sitting in four different leaning
positions in a Swaged Legged Chair;
photo 1958 *by Rooks Photography.*

Nelson Swaged Leg Chair: white arm chair of
two pieces of molded fiberglass connected
with metal tubing, on a metal swaged base;
photo 1958 *by Rooks Photography.*

Swaged Leg Chair: two piece molded fiberglass
armchair, open between the seat and back, with
seat cushion, on metal swaged legs; photo 1961
by Rooks Photography.

AVAILABLE ALSO AS FLIP TOP EXTENSION
TABLE. EXTENDS TO 108" LONG.
(USES EDGE HINGE FOR FLIP TOP)

OILED
WALNUT

COLORED PANELS

WHITE MICARTA.

AVAILABLE IN OILED WALNUT OR
WHITE FORMICA. ALL EDGES ARE
OILED WALNUT.

OILED
WALNUT

OILED WALNUT

CHROME
LEGS
(Bright)

CHROME (bright)

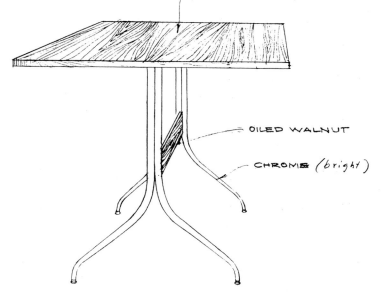

DRAWER FRAMES CONTAINING
FORMED PLASTIC DRAWERS FOR
PENCILS ETC. ENVELOPES AND
STATIONARY.

SIZE: 39"W 28½D 33¾H

SIZE: 54"L 36"W 28½H
(SEE DRAWING#475A TABLE 1)

EXTENDED FLIP TOP
108"L 36"W 28½H

SEE DRAWING (475-1)

Drawing for Swaged Leg Home Desk.

Drawing for Swaged (spelled swedged) Leg Square Table.

(To be discont'd.)

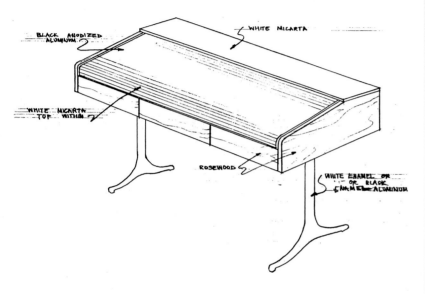

BLACK ANODIZED ALUMINUM

WHITE MICARTA

WHITE MICARTA TOP WITHIN

ROSEWOOD

WHITE ENAMEL OR OR BLACK ENAMEL ALUMINUM

W = 24"   H = 34"   L = 42"

DRWG.   296B8 297
316
317
338

Above:
Drawing for Roll Top Desk.

Right:
Action Office I Roll Top Desk with a foot rail, blue sides, and chromed legs, the wood tambour top partly rolled; photo 1964.

114

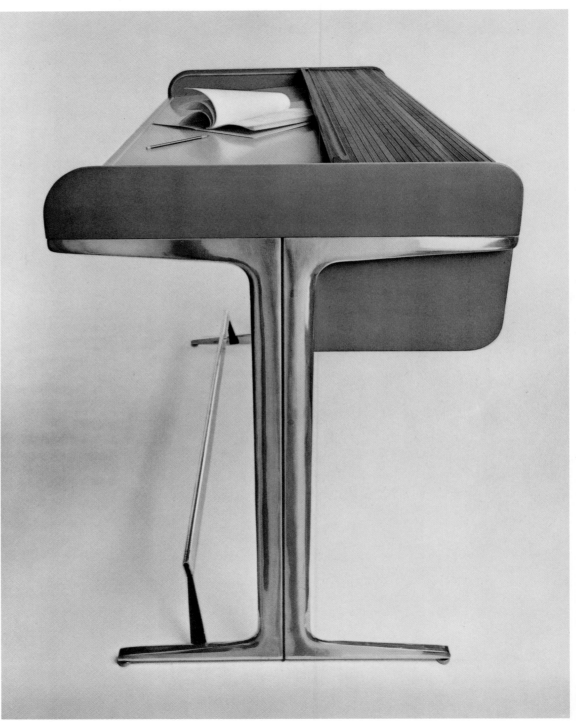

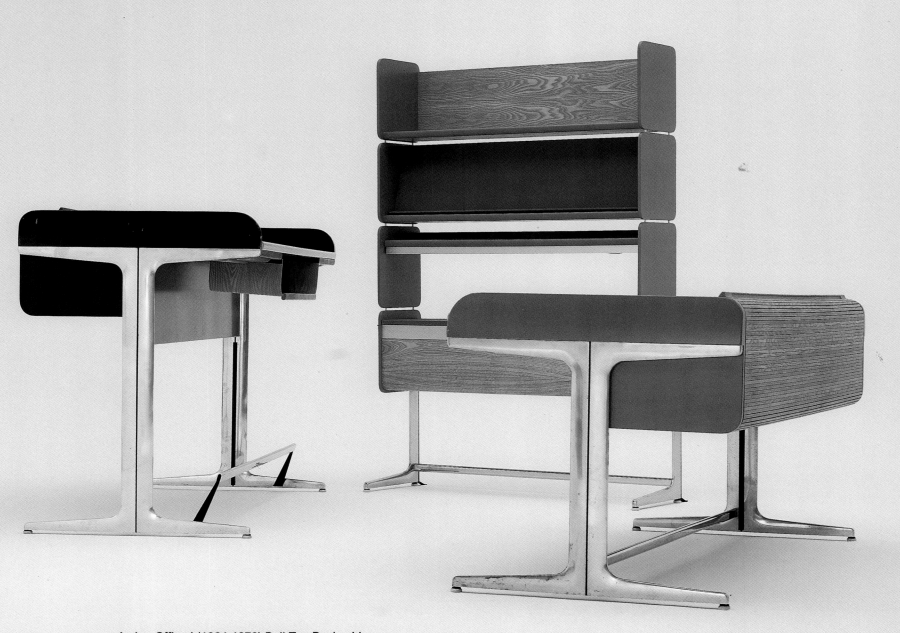

Action Office I (1964-1970) Roll Top Desk with
other items with aluminum trestle bases.

CATINARY CHAIR

DWG NO. 631

Drawing for Catenary Chair.

Nelson Catenary Group: four Catenary Seats and a
glass top Coffee Table; photo 1963 *by Baltazar Korab*.

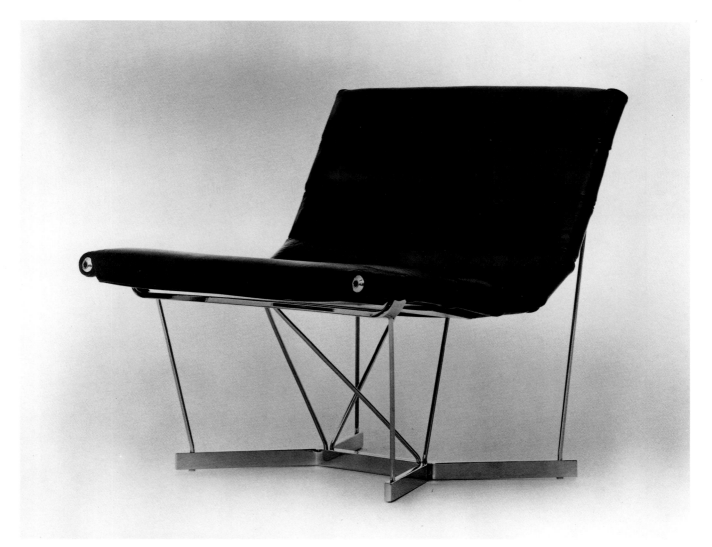

Catenary Seat; photo 1963 *by Baltazar Korab.*

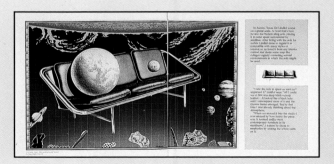

Nelson Sling Sofa (1964 -): brightly polished chrome plated steel tubing frame and base, black leather upholstery on urethane foam cushions, neoprene and reinforced rubber webbing supports slings, stainless steel adjustable glides, 87" length; part of Herman Miller for the Home collection.

Insert:
Sling Sofa in *Reference Points*.

Nelson Cube Group seating, 1967-1974.

Modular Seating (1956-1978): red upholstered Benches, Single Chairs, and Three and Four Seat Couches; photo 1973 *by Earl Woods.*

Noguchi with one of his sculptures; photo given to Herman Miller by Miho Tomoko, c. 1985.

Chapter 3

Isamu Noguchi

Isamu Noguchi (1904-1988)

Isamu Noguchi was born in Los Angeles. His father was a well-known Japanese poet and his mother was a teacher from New York. He lived with his family in Japan from age two until 1918 when his mother sent him to school in Indiana. From 1922 to 1924 he studied medicine at Columbia University, although he had wanted to be an artist. When his mother returned to New York in 1923, she advised him to pursue his real interests, so Noguchi began to seriously study and practice sculpture. He was awarded a Guggenheim Fellowship and studied with Constantin Brancusi in Paris 1927-1928. Noguchi traveled and studied abroad, returning to the United States in 1932. His major sculpture commissions were often associated with architecture, such as a large overdoor panel for the Associated Press Building in New York, a 70-foot colored cement wall sculpture in Mexico, and sculptural panels for the SS Argentina.

His first furniture design, in 1939, was for a rosewood and glass table in the Biomorphic style for Conger Goodyear, president of the Museum of Modern Art. Noguchi was recruited by Herman Miller and designed a similar table with a freeform sculptural base and biomorphic glass top in 1947.

In 1954 he designed a chromed steel Rocking stool and other pieces for Knoll, as well as furniture for Alcoa. Lamp design was another mid-century interest, and in 1948 he designed a simple three-legged cylinder lamp for Knoll. This led to his series of Akari lights made in Japan. These paper spheres, sculptural versions of traditional Japanese paper lamps, were produced for 25 years.

The 1948 Herman Miller catalog featured Noguchi's Chess Table in plywood and cast aluminum with plastic inserts in the top. The top revolved to open two pockets in the casting below it and it came with an ebonized finish. The other piece was his now-classic coffee table described in the catalog as "sculpture-for-use" and "design for production." The base, carved from solid wood, consists of two identical parts. "When one is reversed and connected to the other by a pivot rod, a base appears which has a smoothly flowing form and an interest rarely found in furniture of any period." The self-stabilizing base supports the heavy plate glass top without the use of connectors. Originally produced in birch, walnut, or cherry, with just two components — wood base repeated in reverse and a glass top — Noguchi's table is considered one of the milestones of twentieth-century furniture design.

Game Table (1948-1949) of amorphically shaped wooden legs and top; the top supported on a laquered cast aluminum shell, has white plastic inlaid dots and slides around to open the wooden pockets that hold pieces; top 28" x 26", height 19 1/2"; photo 1950 *by Michael Booth.*

Noguchi Dining Table and four Stools, each with two metal tube legs and one carved wooden plank leg, nicknamed the Fin or Rudder Table and Fin or Rudder Stool and produced in limited quantities for a short time; table top 50" x 30", height 26"; stool height 17-1/4"; photo 1950 *by Rooks Photography.*

Noguchi Table (1948-1973): of two curved solid walnut or ebonized walnut legs that interlock to form a tripod for self stabilizing support, with a 3/4" thick clear plate glass top in a biomorphic shape, reissued in 1984 and in the Herman Miller for the Home line; top 50" x 30", total height 15 3/4".

Insert: Graphic of the Noguchi Table in *Reference Points.*

In 1965 the thickness of the plate glass top was decreased from 7/8" to 3/4". Base dimension also changed, because overall height went from 15" to 15 3/4". Cherry bases were only made in the first year or so of production; birch bases were made between c. 1947 and 1955. A limited edition of about 480 was produced in 1980.

Part Two

Designers of other Herman Miller
classics — past, present, and future

Rohde, c.1934.

Chapter 4

Gilbert Rohde

Gilbert Rohde (1894-1944)

Gilbert Rohde was a pioneer industrial designer and key figure in the introduction of modern design in the United States. Born in New York City, he learned to work with wood at the cabinetmaking shop of his father Max Rohde, an Eastern Prussian immigrant. A precocious and multi-talented child, Rohde later received formal education in woodworking and mechanics at high school in the Bronx. He then apprenticed to a photographer, worked as a reporter and political cartoonist for the *Bronx News*, and did free lance furniture advertisements for Sloane's and Macy's department stores. In 1923 he worked full-time as a furniture illustrator for Abraham & Strauss department store in New York. In 1927, while traveling in Europe, Rohde was married to Gladys Vorsanger of New York City in Paris. He became acquainted with the Bauhaus and then returned home and opened an industrial design office in New York in 1929 and produced his own furniture. Rohde was among the first to make and sell tables with chromed tubular metal legs and Bakelite tops. He and Gladys had two children but were divorced in 1940; the following year Rohde married Peggy Ann Kruelski of Brooklyn, New York in Santa Fe.

Rohde had a particularly important role in introducing modern design at Herman Miller, which started the company in a totally new direction beginning in 1930. Before he came to Herman Miller, the company specialized in case goods in historic reproduction styles. Since Rohde's seating furniture required upholstery, the work had to be sent out to upholstery specialists until Herman Miller formed an in-house upholstery shop. In addition to seating, Rohde is known for his innovative modular units, especially sectional sofas and storage units, and he also introduced the company's first

Rohde, c. 1935.

126

metal furniture. Of greater significance, Rohde brought Herman Miller into the office furniture business with his Executive Office Group (EOG).

Rohde also designed furniture for John Widdicomb, Thonet, Brown-Saltzman, Kroehler, Lloyd, Valentine Seaver, Valley Upholstery, the Z stools and other chromed metal furniture for Troy Sunshade in Troy, Ohio in the 1930s, and a line of indoor-outdoor furniture for Heywood-Wakefield in 1930. Other items included clocks for Howard Miller, water coolers, boilers, pianos, stokers, and gas ranges; exhibits included the "Design For Living" house at the 1933 Chicago World's Fair, the Texas Centennial, the San Francisco Golden Gate Exhibition, and several installations at the 1939 New York World's Fair. He headed the industrial design program at the New York School of Architecture from 1939 to 1943.

As Hugh De Pree wrote, Rohde had the ability to teach, and De Pree had the ability to learn. What De Pree learned was 1) the designer must have absolute control over the design; 2) materials must be respected for their inherent qualities; and 3) the manufacturer must produce furniture of the day and not copy antiques. In the 1930s, under Rhode's direction, Herman Miller became the first company in the United States to mass produce modern furniture. (De Pree 41)

The relationship between Rohde and Herman Miller began "on a hot day in July, 1930" as Hugh's father D.J. De Pree recalled. Rohde asked for $1,000 to design a modern bedroom set (the usual fee at the time was between $100 and $300) but settled for a three percent royalty after the furniture was sold (because Herman Miller allegedly didn't have the cash for a fee). He specified utter simplicity without surface enrichment, carving, or moldings. This was quite a departure from Herman Miller's usual carved and marble-topped case goods. An unadorned surface required precision,

because carving and moldings were commonly used to conceal imprecise construction. The idea intrigued De Pree, as did Rohde's philosophy — that furniture should be space-saving, multi-purpose, and utilitarian. "It was clearly the beginning of a new direction for the Herman Miller Furniture Company. Gilbert Rohde elevated our thinking from selling merely furniture to selling a way of life" (De Pree 16). When the large New York furniture retailer, Ludwig Bauman and Company, bought twelve sets of Herman Miller furniture that Rohde had designed, his future looked bright. He continued to make significant contributions to both Herman Miller and the American furniture industry, including the introduction of sectional or unit furniture, especially the sectional sofa, a Living-Sleeping-Dining group which introduced the idea of multi-use furniture, and the Executive Office Group in which fifteen pieces could combine to make 400 different groupings.

By 1935 Rohde suggested in a letter that the company should begin concentrating on modern, even if it meant dropping the entire traditional line. The following year, a decision was made to cease production of period reproductions and switch to high quality modern furniture. De Pree agreed that it seemed dishonest to copy historic pieces and to fake finishes to give an antique look. Yet, "this decision had to be made in a marketing climate of apathetic stores and a lack of vision among most of our contemporaries in the industry" (18). In order to reach the people who were willing to live with modern design, Herman Miller opened a New York City showroom in 1941. It was a turning point for the company. When Rohde died in 1944, they were already committed to modern design and only needed the right successor to the man who had introduced it. They found George Nelson.

Rohde dining room furniture: drop leaf table with extended leaves and two drawers and a door in the center; upholstered wood chairs; mahogany cabinets matching the table; photo 1939.

Rohde living room furniture: two East India laurel bookcases along
the wall; four-sectional seating; cylindrical coffee table with round
glass top, wood bottom, and half cylinder side; photo 1934.

Rohde Executive Office Group (EOG), c. 1942.

Rohde bedroom furniture: vanity with three attached mirrors and a curved leather-lined leg hole; three-cushioned curved vanity seat; overstuffed lounge chair next to a bean-shaped glass table with glass tube legs; photo 1939.

Rohde bedroom furniture: two bow-front cabinets and a rectangular cabinet with three inlaid horizontal stripes; designed in 1933 for the World's Fair; photo 1981.

Chapter 5

Alexander Girard

Girard in front of
shelves of fabric
samples; photo
1966 *by Jon Naar.*

Alexander Girard (1907-1993)

Born in New York, Alexander Girard grew up in Florence, Italy. At age 22 he graduated from the Royal Institute of British Architects in London; two years later, in 1931, he graduated from the Royal School of Architecture in Rome, and, in 1935, from New York University. He was a registered architect in New York, Michigan, Connecticut, and New Mexico. Girard opened offices in Florence, Santa Fe, and New York in 1932 and in Detroit in 1937, where he practiced architecture and interior design.

Commissions included design of automobile interiors for Ford Motor Co. and interiors and radio cabinet designs for Detrola Corp. In 1938 he designed his own home in Grosse Pointe, Michigan and filled it with folk art from around the world, the inspiration for all of his future designs. In 1949 Girard organized the exhibition "For Modern Living" for the Detroit Institute of Arts, which brought him national acclaim.

He joined Herman Miller in 1950 and became the first director of design for the new Textile Division as well as director of upholstery in 1952. Girard developed new weaves, prints, and color lines. He designed the Herman Miller Showroom in San Francisco in 1958, the Herman Miller Textiles & Objects Shop in New York in 1961, and in 1967 introduced the Girard Group furniture. His bold and colorful graphics were silk-screened on to Environmental Enrichment Panels and used in Herman Miller's Action Office in the 1970s. In 1956, Girard collaborated with Charles Eames to produce the documentary film in Mexico, "Day of the Dead." He organized the exhibit "Textiles and Ornamental Arts of India" at the Museum of Modern Art in New York in 1954. In 1965 the Indian government commissioned Eames and Girard to design the Memorial Exhibition for Nehru. He collaborated again with Eames for the Latin-American theme restaurant, La Fonda del Sol, in the Time-Life Building in New York. Girard designed the interior — from the menus and matchbooks to the tile floors and walls — while Eames designed the La Fonda Chairs. Girard developed a corporate identity program for Braniff International Airways in 1964 which included differently colored aircraft and a series of textile designs for the aircraft seating.

Although his individual projects designing restaurants, public places, exhibitions, and his work for a major airline brought him media coverage and widespread recognition, his work for Herman Miller was consistently creative over an extended period. He was a master of surprise with an uncanny ability to fit pieces together to form a meaningful whole. Hugh De Pree wrote, "Sandro Girard had the same drive for quality as Charles Eames, but with even more concern for detail" (De Pree 50). And "Alexander Girard taught us that business ought to be fun, that part of the quality of life was joy, excitement, and celebration" (59).

His wife Susan Girard was also involved in his design and collecting. They lived in Santa Fe for forty years where they put together an enormous folk art collections from their travels. They had two children, a daughter and a son, who also resided in Santa Fe. The Girard Foundation was established in Santa Fe in 1961, an international collection of over 100,000 pieces of folk art including toys and other objects. In 1978 the Girard Foundation was donated to the State of New Mexico, and the Girard Wing was added to the Museum of International Folk Art in Santa Fe. In 1981 the Girards received the Governor's Award for outstanding contribution to Fine Arts in New Mexico.

Opposite:
Rolls of textiles; photo
1977 *by Earl Woods.*

Group of tables and ottomans upholstered in Girard fabric, all on metal bases; photo 1967.

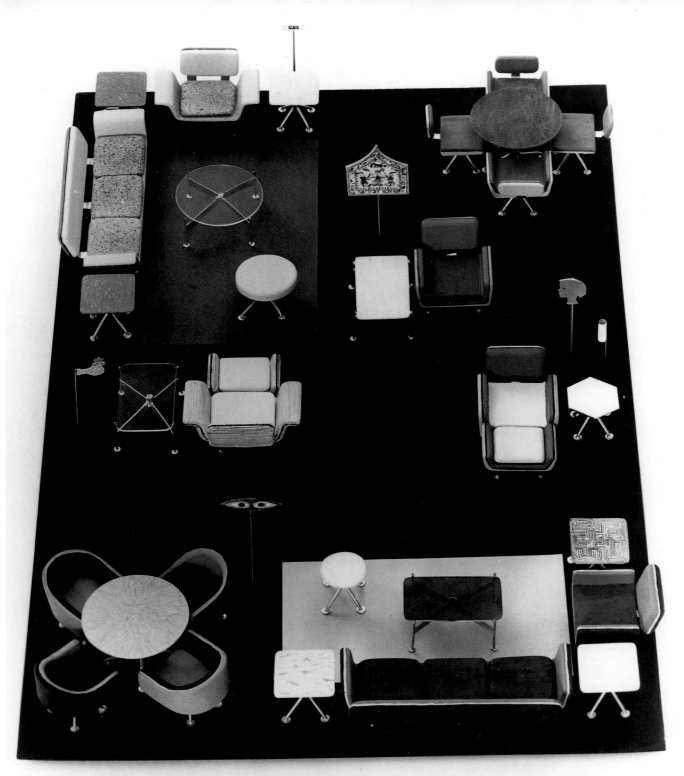

Bird's-eye view of Girard
furniture: sofas, chairs,
ottomans, and tables.

Environmental Enrichment
Panel of "Palace," a black
design on tan background;
photo 1971 *by Earl Woods.*

138

Environmental Enrichment Panel of "Triple Eyes," three pairs of purple (or black) and white eyes with pink and green accents; photo 1971 *by Earl Woods.*

139

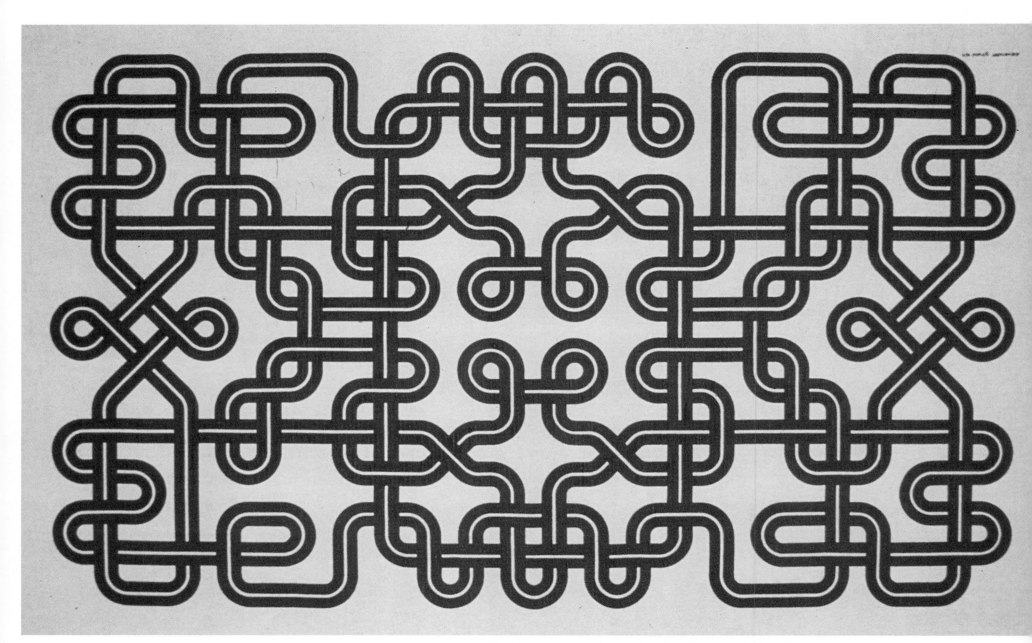

Environmental Enrichment Panel of "Knot," a black and tan woven
knot design on white background; photo 1971 *by Earl Woods.*

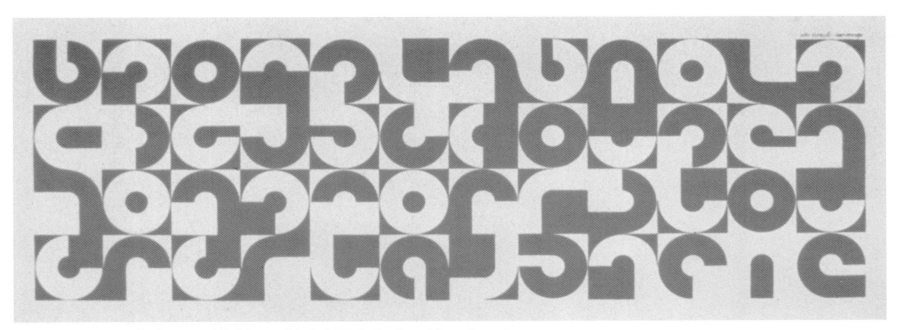

Environmental Enrichment Panel of "Circle Sections A," a pattern of
positive-negative circle sections on squares; photo 1971 *by Earl Woods.*

Chapter 6

Robert Propst

Robert Propst (b. 1921)

Propst was born in Sterling, Colorado and grew up on a cattle ranch. He studied chemical engineering at the University of Colorado, but soon changed his major to fine arts and graduated with a B.A. in 1943. From 1946 to 1948 he headed the Art Department at Tarleton College in Dublin, Texas. He returned to the University of Colorado to earn an M.F.A. degree in 1950, when he also formed the Propst Company in Denver. Propst, like other good designers, saw design as problem solving, and his art and technical background, combined with his focused imagination, enabled him to take design to the level of invention. Propst attracted the attention of Herman Miller with a series of ingenious furniture component connectors. After visiting Propst's studio in Boulder, Colorado, Herman Miller's management became interested in his research, which led to his significant achievements as head of the Herman Miller Research Corporation. In 1964 he won the Best Collection of the Year Award from *Home Furnishings Daily*, in 1970 the American Institute of Interior Designers presented him with the Annual International Design Award, and in 1972 the Institute of Business Designers gave him a Distinguished Service Citation. His work was represented in two exhibitions in 1975: *The Design Process at Herman Miller* at the Walker Art Center in Minneapolis, Minnesota; and *A Modern Consciousness — D.J. De Pree/Florence Knoll* at the Smithsonian in Washington, D.C. In 1976 Propst received the *Design Review* Industrial Design Award, and in 1977 his work was included in a design exhibit at the Centre National d'Art et De Culture Georges Pompidou. In 1985 the Action Office system was named "Best Design of the Past 24 Years" by the International Council of Societies of Industrial Design.

Propst; photo 1979.

Action Office

In 1960 Herman Miller formed the Herman Miller Research Corporation under the direction of Robert Propst. Though their mission was to find and solve problems outside the furniture industry, the first really major project was the office. Before attending to the physical environment, Propst was interested in learning about the ways people work in an office. He listened to what architects had to say, and he also consulted mathematicians, behavioral psychologists, and anthropologists.

By the early 1960s it had become clear that the radical change taking place in the office, as well as outside it, was occurring at a radical rate. Society had suddenly moved from needing more information to having too much information, and the physical environment had failed to accommodate the change. Propst characterized the historic attitude as, "Bring me more information, I will always know what to do with it, I can send it away to store and retrieve at will." In the pre-computerized world of the 1960s, not only was there too much information, it was often repetitive and redundant, out of date by the time it was printed, too specialized, and/or of low quality. A good deal of this new flood of information flowed through the office.

An extraordinary variety of tasks are performed in the office. Yet, historically, rather than vary the facilities according to the task, the tendency has been to standardize the environment, leaving the only variations oriented toward status. This is based on what is called reductive management, "a process of ordering and forbidding as a means to assure performance....Ultimate knowledge lies at the top, independence is discour-

aged, and mistakes call for penalties." The opposite point of view regards each individual as a potential decision maker and manager. "Performers at any level need challenge and encouragement to gain top performance." But when Propst wrote this, his contemporary office system was totally reductive and suffered from "rigidity, lack of delegation, pyramidal management, clogged communication channels, ponderous decision making, and tends to smother creativity and innovation."

Not only was there too much information placed on workers' desks and laps, much of the printed material was never read. With more than could possibly be processed, let alone remembered, the information became counterproductive. Though the mind is capable of dealing with huge amounts of information, it must be in manageable units. Smaller parcels are easier to process and remember, so material must be systematized in order to be useful. It followed that a concept as simple as the physical office environment could contribute to the process of information management.

There were other issues around the dysfunctional office. The body, as well as the mind, had been badly treated. Just as the mind needs variety and exercise, the body becomes overly stressed if limited to only one continuous activity. In the office, this activity is sitting. Again, the physical office facility problem could become part of the solution.

Placement of this facility also mattered more than had been formerly realized. Propst observed that "office planning has frequently treated human beings as a hydraulic quantity of sideless, senseless particles. These moveable particles are arrangeable to the best advantage of a geometry submissive to the architectural statement or simply a desire for nonobjective order." The open office grid plan with row after row of rectangular desks and unrectangular people afforded neither privacy nor involvement. "One of the regrettable conditions in present day offices is the tendency to provide a formula kind of sameness for everyone." Yet office workers require both privacy and interaction, depending in which of their many responsibilities they happen to be involved. The existence of ample information does not imply ample communication.

Propst and the Research Division developed a plan, and George Nelson's Office designed the components of what was called Action Office I (AO-1), introduced in 1964. Herman Miller salespeople called it another marshmallow sofa — beautiful, exciting, and it didn't work. The parts were difficult to assemble, and the cost was too high. Nevertheless, Nelson won the Alcoa Award for the design of AO-1 and apparently neglected to mention Propst's work.

So the Nelson Office and the Propst Research Division went back to the drawing board — or two separate drawing boards — and evidently spent more energy on disagreement than on interaction. Ultimately, Nelson was taken off the project.

Propst learned that in order to improve the state of the American office and its workers, the main issues to address are 1) organization of information; 2) organization of people; and 3) organization of facilities. And once a new system is in place to address these needs, the only constant variable is change. In other words, the only thing that we can predict with absolute certainty is that everything will change. This does not mean that anything we do will not matter; on the contrary, it means that everything we do will matter. But in order to accommodate this inevitable change, we must prepare for it.

In 1968 the company introduced Propst's Action Office 2 (AO-2), a facility based on change. It is an environment designed to accommodate change by its built-in flexibility and adaptability. He called it the "forgiving principle" and wrote, "we must be allowed to change our minds. We must be allowed to respond to errors as they emerge. And this forgiving should not impose significant cost or delay on the user." Change must also be graceful. "When we think of alternatives to ponderous change, we are worried about living a perpetually temporized life in jerry-built, junky facilities." This graceful change must also be well planned and quickly expedited. The obsolescence so apparent with information is apt to slip into the physical plant as well.

Awareness of goals, careful planning, and the use of the right tools for the job must all be considered and must be interdependent. Planning must serve both the organization and the individual. Focus must be on communication — networks of what Propst identifies as 1) general information, 2) instructional information, and 3) opinion.

In order to provide the most efficient physical space for communication, the facility must provide both enclosure and access. Until Propst's work, the choice was for either an open system of desks lined up in a space or a closed system of "bull pens" of individual enclosed offices. Propst found a third alternative — neither all open nor all closed. His premise recognized that people are more comfortable and therefore more productive with a territorial enclave, and that they are uncomfortable in totally open space. Yet people also require vista, a view of the outside. The concept of "backup" is a two or three sided vertical division that defines territory and affords privacy without hindering the ability to view or participate. This wall unit that serves as the basis for office organization can have other functions and other advantages.

The Action Office 2 is based on the mobile wall-like element that defines the space. This unit also supports multiple work station functions, many of which can now be vertically oriented. The panels provide selective visibility or enclosure and support a collection of human-scale, standardized, interchangeable, and versatile components called work surfaces, shelves, drawers, covers, and counter caps. That's it. These simple very basic components are do-it-yourself building blocks that enable any office worker to become his or her own designer, builder, and manager of a personalized and functional space. "With complete assembly agreement and simplicity, the fewest possible parts [serve] the maximum depth of functionality." They also reduce the square footage requirement by utilizing the vertical surface for storage, privacy, and display, which can be total or just enough to prevent losing information, such as in visible folders. Even in the case of the earlier Action Office I, Propst had observed that there is a direct relation between seeing objects and taking action on them. Providing surface space for single layers of paper was one way to insure visibility.

The surface aspects of Action Office were the easiest for other manufacturers to copy, especially since these surfaces intentionally lacked any visual distinction. When author Ralph Caplan met with designers from a competitor in the office system business, he hung up his jacket. It fell down, so Caplan hung it up again...and again, then asked, "How come it keeps falling down?"

"I know why," one of the designers answered. "The coat hook is the only part of this entire system that we didn't rip off from Herman Miller" (Caplan 84).

Items that are more desirable out of sight, like electrical wiring, can be hidden in the panels. Acoustical privacy can be adjusted, lighting is built in and flexible, and signage is a part of the system. The option of using both sitting and standing work station areas relieves the problem of being overly sedentary. Propst understood that there is a direct relation between "modest but definite whole body motion" and "mental fluency and alertness" (Hamilton 27). The office that compels workers to sit all day in one posture sees a drop in work capacity. Action Office, on the other hand, is designed to compel the worker to move frequently.

In addition, portable furniture can be wheeled around to serve needs of formal or informal meetings, and visitors can sit around an uncompromised neutral surface that is brought into the work station or to another location. Like the overly specialized species that becomes extinct when its environment changes, the rigid office environment becomes dysfunctional with new situations, information, technology, or people. The Action Office 2 was designed to be so generalized that it could adapt physically as its users grew and changed.

Propst's interest in health care paralleled his dedication to office efficiency. While continuing to head the Herman Miller Research Corporation, he introduced Coherent Structures, Co/Struc, to the market in 1971. Co/Struc is a system of highly mobile containers, frames, carts, and rails designed to streamline the service functions of the hospital through coordination with its architecture. Propst's other projects included classroom and dormitory environments. According to Hugh De Pree, Propst's ideas and concepts "changed Herman Miller, changed the industry, and changed the way millions of people work in the office, the hospital, laboratory and factory. He left all of that, and a legacy of research. Bob Propst made a difference" (De Pree 102-103).

Men working in an early Action Office; photo 1964.

Graphic for 1969 Action Office 2, by John Manez.

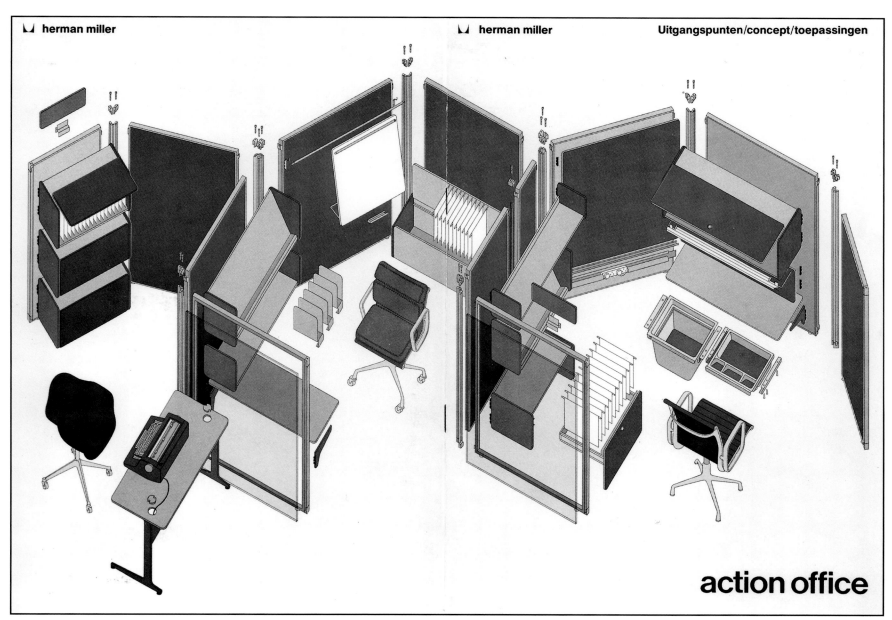

action office

Isometric drawing of Action Office.

Action Office 2,
c. 1969 as shown
in 1985 *AIGA
Annual.*

Jack Kelley.

Chapter 7

Jack Kelley

*I won't tolerate anything that doesn't work on a sailboat, so
why would I tolerate anything that doesn't work in the office?*

Jack Kelley (b. 1932)

Jack Kelley is an avid sailor. The well-designed functional and aesthetically pleasing sailing craft embodies all of his abilities and aspirations — the combination of utility and elegance, the relationship between materials and function, good design distilled to its essence. His studio is in a century home with its own inherently good design and attention to detail. He resides in Spring Lake, Michigan with his wife Joanne, and they have two grown sons, Jeffrey and Michael.

Kelley earned a B.S. in Industrial Design from the University of Michigan in 1962 and immediately joined the Herman Research Division in Ann Arbor, Michigan as a research associate under the direction of Robert Propst. Significant achievements included the Action Office System under Propst in 1968 and the Action Environment (Hospital Supply Delivery System), also under Propst, in 1970, when he became Vice President of Herman Miller Research Corp. In 1974 Kelley was named Director of the Herman Miller Systems Development Group. He became Director of Design & Development, Health Science Division in 1976, and Herman Miller's Corporate Product Design Director in 1979.

Kelley established Studio 222 in Grand Haven, Michigan in 1983 (it moved to Spring Lake in 1988). In 1984 he introduced Ethospace interiors with Bill Stumpf. He designed the Scooter keyboard stand in 1986, and Action Office Series 2 in 1987. Other designs include: the Ethospace nurse's station (for Milcare, Inc.) in 1989; Modular cart system (Milcare) in 1990; 6000 series desk system (for Meridian, Inc.) in 1991; Flex-Edge work surfaces in 1993; Arrio freestanding systems furniture in 1996; and Systems Bridge wall in 1997.

In addition to his work at Herman Miller, Kelley designed office and health care products for Fairfield, Inc. in Tampa, Florida, Nevers Industries, Inc. in Minneapolis, Minnesota, and Sligh Furniture Co. in Holland, Michigan. Awards include: *ID* magazine's Best Designs in 20 Years for his Action Environment in 1973; IDSA Design Excellence Award for Action Laboratory in 1982; IBD Gold Award for Ethospace in 1985; the Roscoe Award for Ethospace in 1985; IDSA Design Excellence Award or Ethospace in 1985; IDSA Worldesign Congress Best Design 1961-1985 for Action Office in 1985; IDSA Design Award for Scooter in 1987; *Corporate Design and Realty Magazine* Award for Scooter in 1987; IBD Design Award for Corridors Desk Group in 1989; *Facility Design & Management Magazine* Best of NeoCon Award for Corridor Wall System in 1990; and *ID* magazine's Annual Design Review Award for Flex-Edge in 1995. Kelley holds more than 45 United States and foreign design patents.

Ethospace

The frame-and-tile wall is the foundation of Ethospace interiors. The steel frames link with one another, while surface tiles simply clip onto the frames. Together the frames, tiles, and top and end caps form a sturdy, 3-1/2 inch wall. Tiles attach to both sides of a frame, so the interior side of a wall can serve specific functions while the exterior coordinates with the overall design scheme of the office area. Without dismantling the frame or disrupting work flow, the function, color, or character of an Ethospace wall can be changed by selectively replacing the tiles. The fabric-covered tiles can be reupholstered on site, either to repair damage or to update the appearance.

What makes Kelley's system desirable is its extreme flexibility — occupants can design the space in any size or shape for degrees of privacy and for specific functions. What makes it really work is its ability to change easily in order to adapt to new needs or simply to change appearance. Ethospace was designed to remedy the loss of identity and control suffered by occupants of ordinary office cubicle space.

Kelley Scooter, portable and adjustable keyboard and other equipment
support, introduced in 1986 and in Herman Miller for the Home.

Scooter in use.

Ethospace interior with Ergon Chairs;
photo 1987 *by Hedrich-Blessing.*

Ethospace interior with Equa Chairs at Herman
Miller Main Site; photo 1987 *by Hedrich-Blessing.*

152

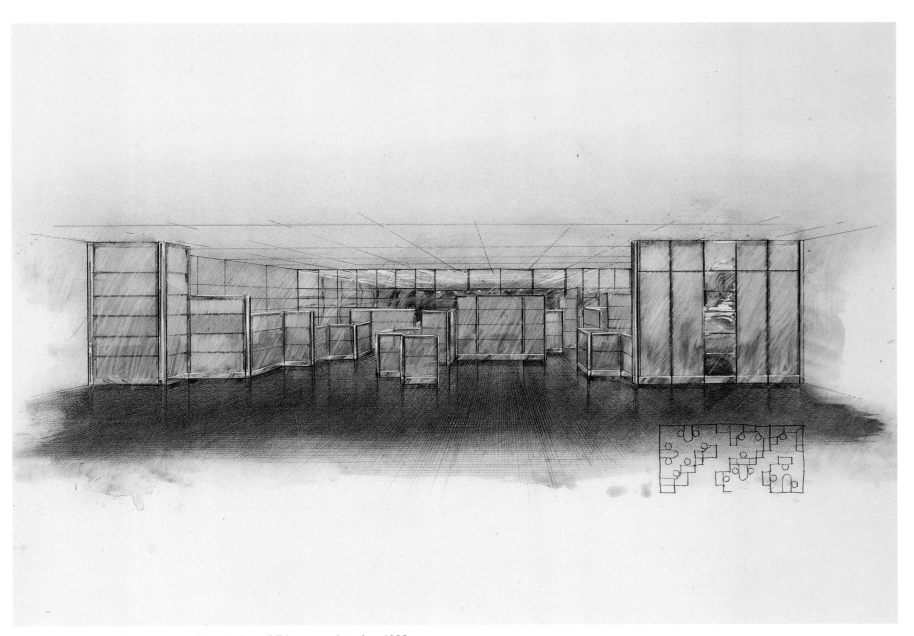

"Grand and expressive entrances" rendering of Ethospace interior, 1986.

Kelley Systems Bridge with Action Office Series 2 and Equa
seating; photo 1997 *by Nick Merrick, Hedrich-Blessing.*

Kelley Systems Bridge with Nelson Pedestal Table and Eames
Lounge; photo 1997 *by Nick Merrick, Hedrich-Blessing.*

Chapter 8

Don Chadwick

Don Chadwick; *photo
Mark Tuschman*.

Don Chadwick (b. 1936)

Don Chadwick became interested in furniture design as a child, when his cabinetmaker grandfather taught him to use handtools. Later, he focused on furniture design and earned a B.A. in Industrial Design at U.C.L.A. in 1959. His resume states, "1954-59 UCLA degree in Industrial Design, the world is larger than L.A." After listening to Charles Eames lecture there, he became optimistic about the contribution furniture design can make in people's lives. Like Eames, Chadwick's California environment seemed to encourage a confident individuality and a curiosity that motivated his design. He established Donald Chadwick and Associates in Santa Monica, California in 1964, and in 1975 formed Chadwick Stumpf and Associates, research and design. He also joined the faculty of U.C.L.A. in 1975.

Chadwick considers Herman Miller his "partner in recklessness." He explains that "Herman Miller isn't afraid to take chances on new ideas. That's why the company's been successful for so long, and that's one reason why it's challenging to work for them." Significant designs for Herman Miller are the Chadwick modular seating in 1974 and C-Forms desks in 1980. In collaboration with Bill Stumpf he also designed the Equa chair in 1984 and the Aeron chair in 1994. Awards include: *ID* magazine's Award for Design Excellence in 1970, '71, '73, and '74; the IBD First Place award for modular seating in 1974; the Governor's Award for Design Excellence at the Design Michigan exhibition in 1977; the IBD Silver Award and IDSA Design Excellence Award for C-Forms in 1980;

the IBD Gold Award for Equa seating in 1984; the Corporate Design and Realty Award for Equa seating in 1985; *Time* magazine's Best of Decade Design for Equa chair in 1990; and selection of the Aeron Chair for the Permanent Collection of the Museum of Modern Art in 1994, the year of its introduction.

Equa Chairs

Don Chadwick and Bill Stumpf worked together for more than five years to develop the design of an "equitable" chair that would fit any office task and any office worker without requiring complicated adjustments. The Equa Chair was introduced in 1984 with a seat and backrest formed by a single piece of molded, glass-reinforced polyester resin. The connection between the shell and the die-cast aluminum base is plainly revealed. The shell flexes in response to subtle body movements, supporting the sitter in almost any posture while allowing the feet to remain flat on the floor when the body tilts back. Equa is available in high or low back models, and the line includes a stool and a guest chair on a rocker or sled base.

In 1983, just before the introduction of the Chadwick-Stumpf Equa Chair, Chadwick was interviewed by Herman Miller archivist Linda Folland. He recalled that in 1977 he met Bill Stumpf on a seating program offshoot. They both realized that chairs needed to be more interactive with the users, more self-adjusting. Office chairs at the time were too complicated and had too many features that weren't being used, so they formulated the following criteria for seating:

1. It should support a person's movements.
2. The basic pivot points in the body were to be ergonomically addressed.

Problems the team sought to solve included:

1. Feet on base to stand.
2. Pelvic pivot leaning back led to shell development to be self-adjusting. It flexes close to the pelvic pivot point. Other chairs force users to arch their backs. Fixed-angle adjustments are allowed by other chairs. Equa is more flexible. It is based on analysis of body movements and moves subtly to respond.
3. How the chair goes together as separate parts. Other seating is not a celebration of form to the extent that Equa is. Equa has only two controls — tension and height.

Options on the Equa Chair:

1. Without tilt.
2. Without arms.
3. Fully upholstered to nonupholstered.
4. High or low back.
5. Stools with adjusting footring in 2 heights.
6. Glides and casters.
7. Sled base.
8. Rocker base.
9. Stacking Chair option still being developed.

Bob Nagelkirk developed the structural integrity of the high and low versions of the shell, the upholstery, hardware, and foam. Bruce Gezon developed the tilt concept, castings, and metal. Don Goeman developed the stool understructure, rocker and sled bases, and two versions of arm pads.

Aeron Chair

"It breaks radically with traditional notions about workplace chairs. It does away with cultural expectations about the comfort of fabric and foam. And it has enough technological materials and ergonomic breakthroughs to keep the Patent Office busy for weeks." (Pearlman).

One of the radical departures taken by the Aeron is in the use of a new mesh-like material called Pellicle, which replaced the more traditional upholstered foam construction. Pellicle always retains its form, prevents pressure on the tailbone and aerates the body. The chair enables weight to be distributed evenly, and the body "floats" on the Pellicle without touching the chair frame.

When asked by *I.D.* magazine in 1995 what he would like to design or redesign, Chadwick answered, "gardening tools."

Chadwick Modular Seating, introduced in 1974; the upholstered molded foam modules come in straight, inside wedge, and outside wedge shapes.

Chadwick Modular Seating.

Chadwick-Stumpf Equa 2 Chair;
photo Dan Van Duinen.

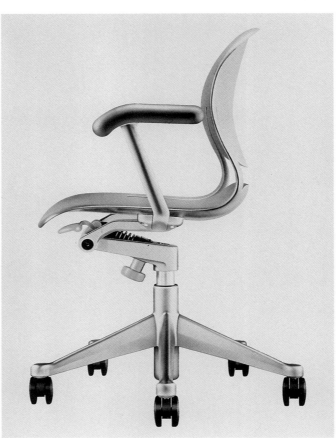

Equa, "A Serious Chair," featured in
the 1984 issue of *Design Quarterly.*

Chadwick-Stumpf Aeron Chair, introduced 1994.
The lightweight and breathable Pellicle material
conforms to the sitter's body, distributes the weight
evenly, and retains its original shape. The Kinemat
tilt allows the body to naturally pivot at the ankles,
knees, and hips; and the two-stage pneumatic lift
provides a wide range of height adjustment. *photo
Nick Merrick, Hedrich-Blessing.*

Bill Stumpf

Design should be like jazz, improvising and discovering, blending the pleasure and pain of life into something wonderful.

Bill Stumpf (b. 1936)

"When his Ergon Chair was introduced, Bill Stumpf observed wryly that 'designing a chair for Herman Miller is like running for Pope'" (Hollington 76) because of the impossible expectations for any chair bearing the Herman Miller name after the Eames era.

Bill Stumpf eventually reached legendary status of his own. He received a B.F.A. in Industrial Design from the University of Illinois in 1959 and an M.S. in Environmental Design from the University of Wisconsin in 1968. He served as a designer for Peter Muller-Munk & Associates and as director of the Advanced Industrial Design Department at the Franklin Division of the Studebaker Corporation, and he taught at the University of Wisconsin and at the Illinois Institute of Technology. He began his association with Robert Propst at the Herman Miller Research Corporation as research director on educational projects at Harlem Prep and Clear Creek schools. He then became vice president of Herman Miller Research Corporation in 1971 and remained until 1973, when he formed Stumpf Associates in Winona, Minnesota. He established Chadwick Stumpf and Associates, research and design in 1977, and now heads William Stumpf & Associates in Minneapolis.

Bill Stumpf; *photo Mark Tuschman*.

His research in ergonomics — the study of the relationship of people to their environments with an emphasis on health, safety, and comfort — resulted in the Ergon Chair in 1976; Equa seating with Don Chadwick in 1984; Ethospace interiors with Jack Kelley in 1984; the Ergon 2 Chair in 1988; the revolutionary Aeron Chair in collaboration with Don Chadwick in 1994; and the Ergon 3 Chair in 1995. He also designed products for Recovery Engineering, Inc., Amtrak, and Forms and Surfaces, Inc.

Stumpf won the ASID best design award for the Ergon chair in 1976, the Design Michigan Award for his Ergon seating in 1977, *ID* magazine's "Designer of the '70s" award in 1979, Certificate of Merit from the Art Directors Club of Los Angeles in 1984, *ID* Annual Review in 1984 and 1985, the IBD Gold Award in for Equa in 1984, the IBD Gold Award in for Ethospace in 1985, the IDSA Design Excellence Award in 1985, the Design Center Stuttgart Award in 1987, *Time* magazine's Best of Decade Design Award for Equa in 1990, the Nissan Award/Fellowship of the Aspen Conference in 1991, and *ID* Top Designers in America Selection in 1993. The Aeron Chair was selected for the Permanent Collection of the Museum of Modern Art in 1994.

He has lectured extensively in the United States and in Europe. His exhibitions include: the Walker Art Center in Minneapolis Minnesota and Cranbrook Academy Museum in Bloomfield Hills, Michigan in 1984; the University of Wisconsin, Milwaukee, and the School of Fine Arts and the STA Gallery in Chicago in 1989; and the Henry Ford Museum in Dearborn, Michigan in 1991. Stumpf's widespread recognition has already elevated his designs to the level of classics.

On work and design:

I work best when I'm pushed to the edge, when I'm at the point where my pride is subdued, where I'm an innocent again. Herman Miller knows how to push me that way, mainly because the company still believes — years after D.J. De Pree first told me — that good design isn't just good business, it's a moral obligation. Now *that's* pressure.

When asked by *I.D.* magazine in 1995 what he would like to design or redesign, Stumpf replied, "a 747 that returns the experience of flight to one and all, à la Norman Bel Geddes's visions of future airplanes in the '30s."

Stumpf Ergon 3 Chair, introduced in 1995; *photo Dan Van Duinen.*

Chadwick-Stumpf Equa Rocker, introduced in 1984, in Herman Miller for the Home; *photo Phil Schaafsma.*

Chadwick-Stumpf Aeron Chair. *photo Nick Merrick, Hedrich-Blessing.*

Ethospace Interiors.

In 1976 Herman Miller introduced the first chair designed to provide "ergonomic" comfort to people in the work place. In 1988, continuing research enabled the original design to evolve, and the Ergon 2 chair was introduced. Designed by Bill Stumpf, the Ergon 2 chair has rounded "waterfall" edges that support without restricting circulation. It has a "pocket that the sitter fits into, and the specially curved back cushion supports the lower back. The sitter can tailor the chair to support his or her size and task with adjustments like seat height, back height, tilt tension, and, on the task model, seat depth and back angle." Ergon 3 followed in 1995.

163

Chapter 10

Tom Newhouse

Tom Newhouse (b. 1950)

When Tom Newhouse was in the ninth grade he already knew that he wanted to be an industrial designer. "I can't remember a time when I wasn't planning, designing, and building. If our class put on a play, I'd build the set. If something broke, I'd fix it. I've always loved to find out how things work." His father was an engineer and his mother an artist, and both contributed to his balance of technical ability and aesthetics.

He graduated from the University of Michigan in 1972 with a B.S. in Industrial Design and began working for Herman Miller. "At an age when most designers might be happy just to have a job, I was picking the brains of some of the established great designers," he admitted. Working in the environment of Charles and Ray Eames, George Nelson, Alexander Girard, and Robert Propst was the most that any young designer could want. After several years as senior designer for facilities, exhibit, and products, he formed his own one-man business, Thomas J. Newhouse Design, in 1978. Working from his home, Newhouse could be near his wife and daughter, have his own workshop, and be away from corporate bureaucracy and distractions. His love for his work and for the freedom to perform it in his own environment has resulted in significant achievements. His Newhouse Group freestanding modular furniture was introduced by Herman Miller in 1987 as an alternative to hanging components in panel systems. He also designed products such as full-height walls for Ethospace, filing systems, an electrical system for Action Office Encore, and Herman Miller exhibitions, including the 1987 London introduction of Ethospace interiors.

Tom Newhouse; *photo Mark Tuschman*.

Awards and recognition for his Newhouse Group furniture include the *ID* Annual Design Review Award in 1987, the Resources Council "Roscoe" Award in 1987, and the IDSA Industrial Design Excellence Award in 1988. Other honors include the Passive Solar Residential Design award by the U.S. Dept. of Housing and Urban Development and U.S. Dept. of Energy in 1978 for his own home, and the Governor's Award at the "Design in Michigan" exhibition in 1977 for his cabin.

Newhouse is committed to designing products and utilizing manufacturing technologies that place the highest priority on preserving the environment. "I have been passionate on this issue for the past twenty-five years and will continue to be," he says. "That's one reason why I love to work with Herman Miller." And that is one reason why Herman Miller loves to work with Tom Newhouse.

Above left:
Dual Newhouse work stations in Ethospace interiors in the Chicago showroom; photo 1990 *by Rich Rutledge.*

Above right:
Newhouse Group Credenza; photo 1987 *by Earl Woods.*

Left:
Newhouse Group Bow-Front Storage; photo 1987 *by Bill Lindhout.*

Chapter 11

Geoff Hollington

Geoff Hollington (b. 1949)

"If you asked me, way back, what's the one company in the world I'd really like to work for, it would have been Herman Miller," Geoff Hollington reflected. He is originally from Hainault, Essex, England, and his first conscious design was an electric guitar, which he started at age thirteen. He earned a B.A. in Industrial Design from the Central School of Art and Design in London in 1971, followed by an M.A. in Environmental Design from the Royal College of Art in London. "By the time I graduated from RCA I had evolved from would-be car stylist, to industrial designer who really wanted to be a sculptor, to interior designer who really wanted to be an architect" (Hollington 15). His office is in London, and he has several important designs in the Herman Miller line: Ethospace support cabinets in 1988; Hollington Chairs in 1989; and the Relay line of free standing office furniture in 1990. Important designs for other companies include reception and dining furniture for Pel in 1979, an office furniture system for G.A. Harvey in 1982, reception seating for Gordon Russell in 1984 , and a prefabricated strong room system for John Tann Ltd. in 1990. His other various designs include everything from telephones to chess computers. In 1988 he won the IBD Gold Award for his Ethospace cabinets and in the same year was elected Fellow of the Royal Society of Arts in England. Hollington won the Industrial Design Excellence Gold Award and the IBD Award for Relay in 1991. In 1993, Industry Forum Design (Germany) presented Relay furniture with the "IF Award for Good Industrial Design."

On offices:
In the '60s and '70s, we tended to think of offices as factories or laboratories. We're moving into a time when we think of offices as places where we can be creative.

On the Hollington Chair:
Perhaps it was a mistake to code-name the chair "Flipper," as we did at first, because of its strange armrests. Things improved a bit when we renamed it "Theo." The aim was to design a work chair with good comfort and ergonomics that was not macho or technical looking; many office chairs have more in common visually with a photo-copier than any kind of furniture (Hollington 68).

On Relay:
I want to affect the end-user by putting joy into the product. Something that lifts the spirit. Something that makes you want to play with the product in some way (quoted in Tetlow 146) ....I'd like people to enjoy the furniture in a sensual way — to enjoy the way it looks and feels (151).

...the design goals had become somewhat paradoxical. The freestanding pieces had to be optimized for workstation-building, but they needed to be as comfortably furniture-like as possible (you could take one home), and they had to be easily movable, so that you could make changes easily, without tools...Added to this, they would need to support computers, wires and cables in a competent but relaxed way (Hollington 86).

Relay is designed to offer the best of both worlds — the freestanding warm furniture that feels almost residential and is more humane than systems, plus compatibility with systems. Individual pieces can be combined with, for example, Ethospace, the Newhouse Group, or other Herman Miller chairs. All desks have waterfall edging in front and bullnose edging in back for easy conferencing, and each piece with a horizontal surface "docks" together for meetings or viewing large documents. Puppy (the faithful companion) is a mobile file cabinet with a top that slides to one side and a drawer that pulls to the other. With Relay, it seems that the company that brought systems to the workplace also found a solution for some of its problems.

Geoff Hollington.

Hollington Chair with low back and leather
upholstery; photo 1989 *by Bill Sharpe.*

Hollington Executive Chair, "Otto;" *photo Bill Sharpe.*

Relay office with all of the Relay furniture products, all in the
Herman Miller for the Home line; photo 1990 *by Roger Hill.*

Relay High Performance Desks, Bookcases, Credenzas, and
Tables in Ethospace interiors frames; *photo James Terkeurst.*

Above:
Relay enclosed Double Pedestal Desk with a Work
Organizer; *photo Bill Sharpe.*

Above right:
Relay Mobile Storage Unit, "Puppy;" *photo Bill Sharpe.*

Right:
Relay Credenza, 36" wide with speckled laminate top,
chestnut base, and black umber base; *photo Bill Sharpe.*

Relay High Performance Desk with a C-Leg in beech
veneer with black umber base; *photo Bill Sharpe.*

Relay piano-shaped End Table used to form
workstation corners or as an accent table, with
either laminate or wood top; *photo Bill Sharpe.*

Bruce Burdick.

The growth of work tools has made the idea of the desk only as a flat surface to write on functionally outmoded. What I wanted was a desk that was responsive to the way an individual works: something that could support performance in the same way that a good pair of running shoes, a fine violin, or skis do; one that could change and grow over time as its users need change; a desk that a designer could specify for 20 different people, with each one being different.

Bruce Burdick (b. 1933)

Burdick is described at Herman Miller as someone who "spends much of his time contemplating and studying the inclinations of primates — both human and simian." He developed the Primate Educational Center of the San Francisco Zoo and believes that zoos should explain the designs of nature to people. Human environments should elucidate human design, and all human design should address what humans need, what we want, how we live, and how we work.

Chapter 12

Bruce Burdick

Burdick was born and raised in Los Angeles. After majoring in Architecture at the University of Southern California, he earned a B.S. in Industrial Design from Art Center College in 1961. While a junior at the Art Center, he worked with Charles Eames at the Eames Office, and after completing school he worked with noted designers John Follis and Herb Rosenthal. He established the Burdick Group in Los Angeles in 1970 and in San Francisco in 1977. He designed and developed traveling exhibits and pioneered a new use of computers in exhibits on economics and nutrition at the Museum of Science and Industry in Chicago. In addition he worked on the design and development of environmental education centers, a museum of oceanography, and the concept planning for the Institute of Automotive Science and History.

His Burdick Group office furniture for Herman Miller is "an elegant but extremely functional alternative to traditional executive furnishings" comprised of "an assemblage of work surfaces, paper handling and storage elements, and electronic equipment supports, located along a structural armature in whatever configuration best suits the way in which people work." It won him the IBD and IDSA design awards in 1980 and one of the five *Time* magazine "Best of 1981" industrial design awards in 1981. Additions to the Burdick Group in 1986 include a peninsula table, large machine table, tool caddie lateral file, and universal keyboard tray. His Spring table, also introduced in 1986, was designed with "a desire for furniture that is more expressive," as well as the desire to bring materials and technology together so that "pleasure and function are inseparable."

Bird's-eye view of Burdick Group office
configuration with round glass-top table.

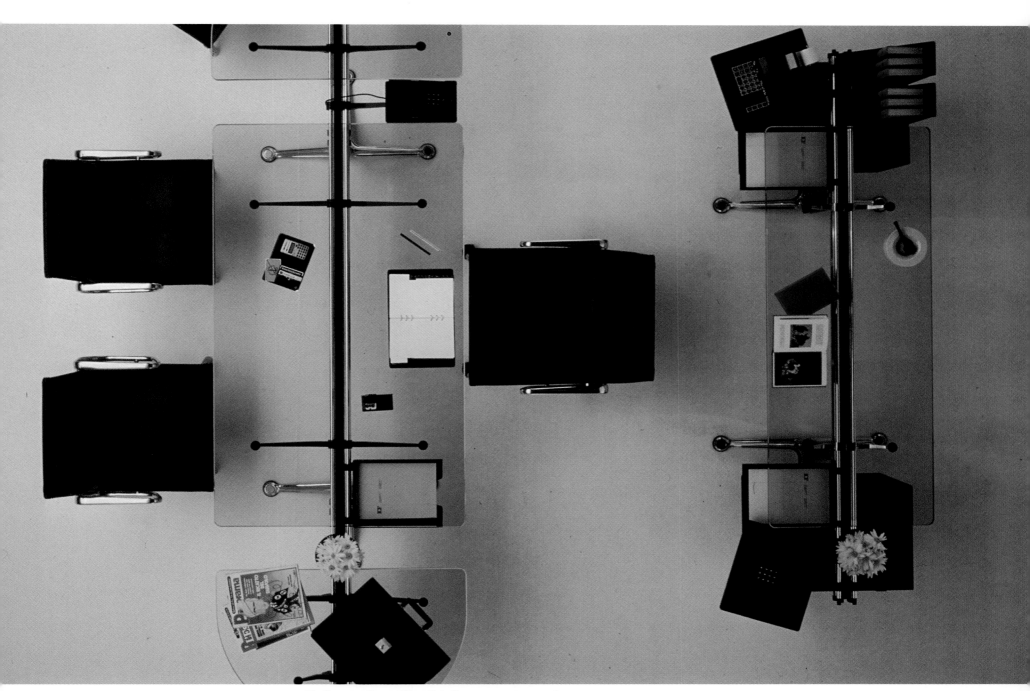

Bird's-eye view of Burdick Group arrangement
with glass-topped table/desk Dining Table.

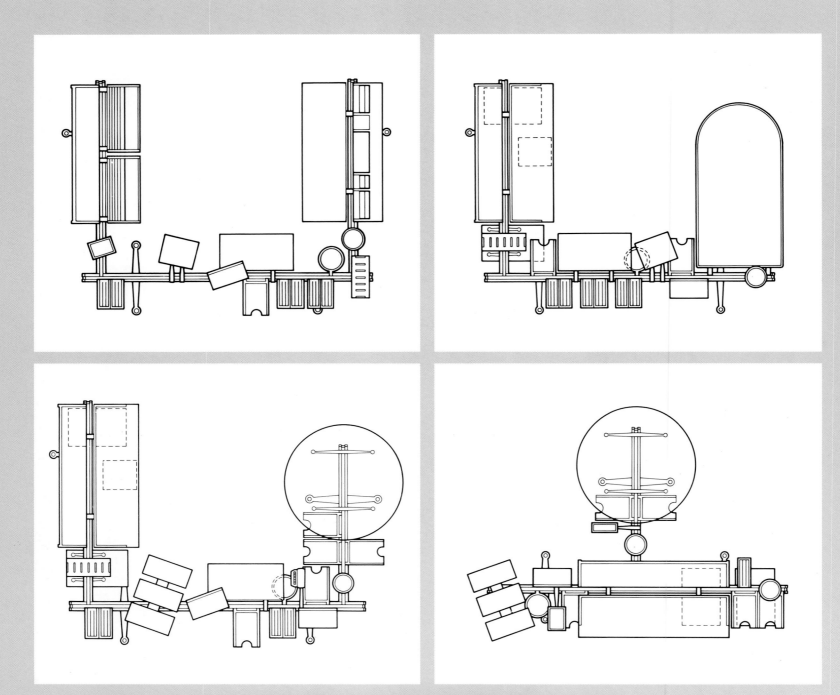

Line drawings of various configurations of Burdick Group pieces.

Burdick Table in office setting.

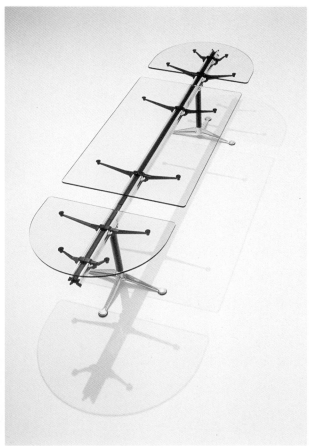

Burdick table/desk Dining Table, introduced in 1981 and in Herman Miller for the Home; *photo Phil Schaafsma*.

Chapter 13

Stephen Frykholm

Stephen Frykholm with photos of Herman Miller employees
in the background, used in the 1985 Annual Report.

Stephen Frykholm (b. 1942)

Although not what one would consider a traditional person, Frykholm's work has been recognized by and exhibited at numerous bastions of respectability, including the Museum of Modern Art in New York, the Renwick Gallery of the National Museum of American Art in Washington D.C., and shows sponsored by the American Institute of Graphic Arts. He earned a B.F.A. from Bradley University, and in 1969, an M.F.A from Cranbrook Academy of Art. Between degrees, Frykholm served in the Peace Corps as a teacher in Nigeria from 1965 to 1967.

As Herman Miller's Creative Director, Frykholm designed a stunning series of posters for the annual Herman Miller picnics from 1970 to 1989, some of which are in the permanent collections of the Museum of Modern Art, the Smithsonian Institute National Museum of Design, the Museum of Decorative Art in Copenhagen, and Musee Des Arts Decoratifs de Montreal. Posters for the years 1971, 1975, 1976, 1977, and 1980 are shown in the *1985 American Institute of Graphic Arts Annual*.. He repeatedly earned recognition and awards from organizations such as the New York Art Director's Club, the American Institute of Graphic Arts, the American Center for Design, and the publications *Communication Arts, Industrial Design,* and *I.D.*

He and his wife, interior architecture designer Nancy Phillips, collaborated on design projects including a stable and indoor arena for their horses. They live in one of their projects outside Grand Rapids, and Frykholm calls his surroundings "a combination of useful design and playful art." His playful, while at the same time serious, attitude toward his work turned out to be a very positive force at Herman Miller, and he brought a new dimension to the way in which products and programs are portrayed. Consequently, Frykholm was honored with Herman Miller's highest award for employee service, the Carl F. Frost Award, in 1986.

SQA

He is currently Chief Creative Officer for Herman Miller subsidiary, Miller SQA. An abbreviation for "Simple, Quick, Affordable," SQA was founded in 1984 in order to recycle used, yet perfectly good, Herman Miller furniture. Clients who wanted new configurations, fabrics, or finishes did not necessarily want or need all new products. So SQA (first called Tradex and then Phoenix Designs) took used furniture and disassembled, reconditioned, reassembled, and resold it. The company added a limited line of new items and used the same method — sophisticated and efficient software, installed into laptop computers in the client's office, is used to prepare the new layout, specifications, details, and costs. Then a sophisticated and efficient team at the new light-filled building completes the job in a fraction of the usual time. Frykholm's move to SQA seems a logical one. Through the years, he has been one of the designers with vision who developed the kind of relationship with the company that maximized the potential of both; in doing so, Frykholm contributed to the image and the quality that make classic Herman Miller.

Picnic

Many of the picnic posters are still available through Herman Miller (from 1990 they were designed by Kathy Stanton), because the graphics have continued to appeal to collectors as well as those affiliated with the company and the picnics. Although the posters began in 1970, the annual company picnic has a longer history. It was held sporadically until after World War II and then became a regular event to celebrate the company and to acknowledge the importance of family and community.

In 1947 attendance was 314, or 97% of the employees. In 1986 approximately 7,000 people attended and consumed more than 6,000 chickens. It first took place at various parks and fairgrounds that were large enough to accommodate thousands of attendees. Then Quincy Jones, the architect of Herman Miller's main building, installed accessible public facilities in the Spine and designed the ponds in front of the building with picnic activities in mind.

In keeping with Herman Miller's tradition of being resourceful and sensitive to the environment, no picnic waste is sent to landfills. All materials used are burnable and nontoxic, and all waste goes directly to the Energy Center boiler. Balloons are no longer distributed, and paper name tags have replaced metal buttons. Participants include employees and their immediate families, contract people, and retirees with ten or more years with the company. Although the tradition continues each year, earlier posters by Frykholm, and more recently by Stanton, continue to celebrate all picnics.

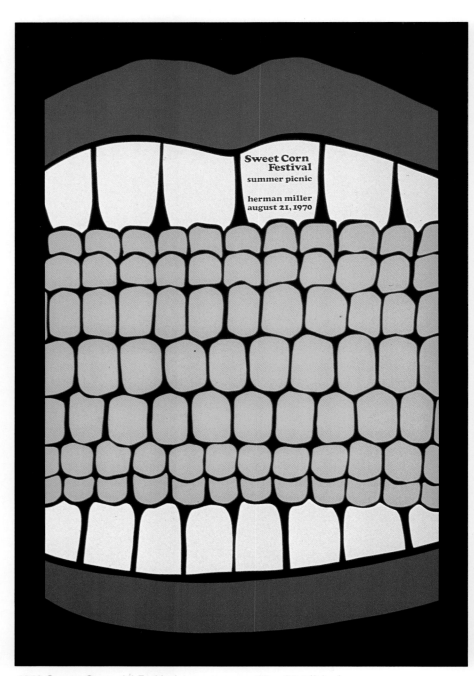

1970 Sweet Corn. All Frykholm posters are 25 x 39-1/2 inches.

1971 Watermelon by Steven Frykholm with Philip Mitchell.

1972 Hot Fudge Sundae.

1973 Hotdog.

1974 Popcorn.

182

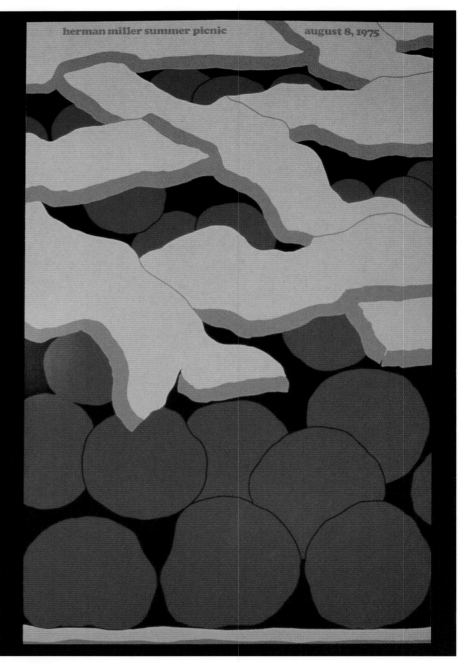

1975 Cherry Pie.
Western style beef and turkey were served to approximately 1,900
Herman Miller employees and retirees at Leisure Acres. Each family
received a gift, and the grand prizes were furniture and trips.

1976 Ham with Pineapple Slices.
About 2,000 people came to Leisure Acres and were entertained by Hickory Creek, the bluegrass band from Benton Harbor. The grand prize was a trip to Hawaii.

1977 Fruit Salad.

1978 Chocolate Cake.
County Fair was the theme at main site in Zeeland, and about 3,800 attended.
The grand prize was a trip for two to Austria on the Herman Miller tour.

1979 Chicken O Grill.
More than 4,000 gathered at main site and listened to the Sweetcorn String Band
and the Herman Miller Band. Grand prizes were $750 and a week paid vacation.

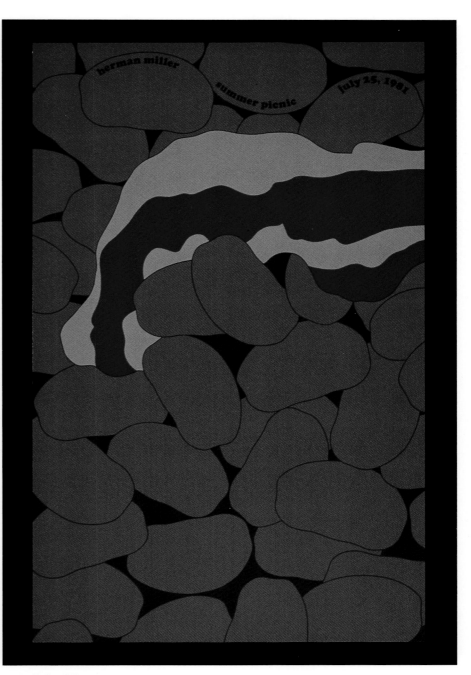

1980 Lemonade.
More than 5,000 gathered again at main site and listened to the Sweetcorn String Band. Exhibits of historical trucks and Herman Miller furniture were popular. The grand prize was an Eames Lounge and Ottoman.

1981 Baked Beans.

185

1982 Seven-Layer Salad.

1983 Ice Cream Cone.

186

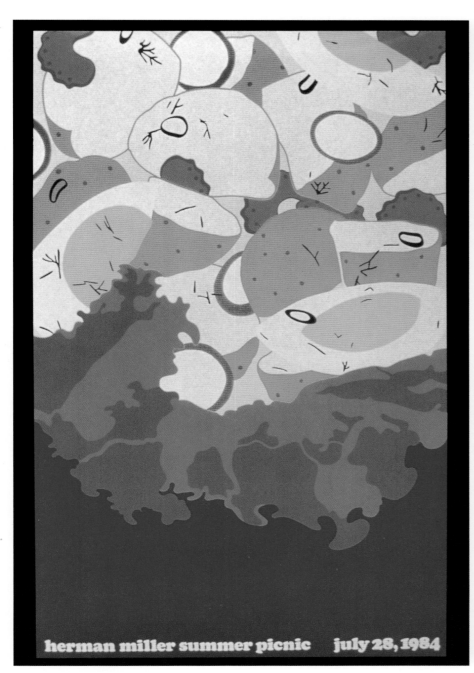

1984 Potato Salad.
More than 5,000 attended.

1985 Red & White Tablecloth

1986 Orange and Lemon Slices.
The theme was Hawaiian for the 7,000 attendees who were offered free karate and aerobic lessons after consuming 6,000 chickens and the traditional home-made peach sundaes. Prizes were a week in Hawaii and $750, a week's paid vacation with $500 spending money, and an Eames Lounge and Ottoman.

1987 Popsicles.
5,000 attendees enjoyed games, hayrides, horse and buggy rides, and ate barbecued chicken and all the trimmings. Popsicles were served for the first time.

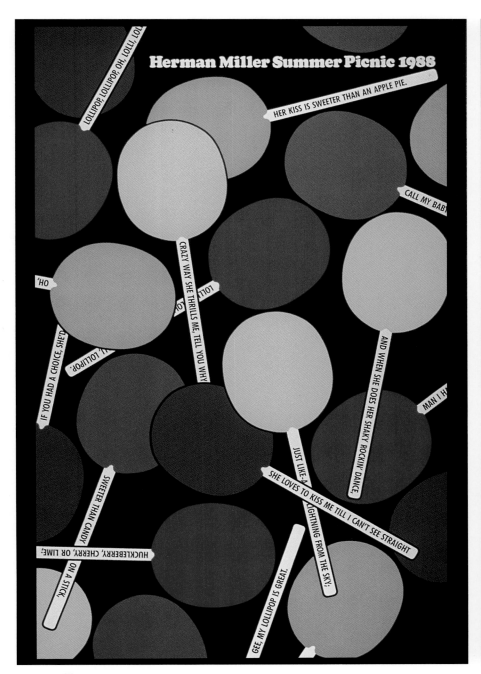

1988 Lollipops.
The 1950s theme included a hula-hoop contest, '50s memorabilia, '50s music, and '50s cars. About 6,600 attended.

1989 Peach Sundae.
Stephen Frykholm's posters were featured in a special display at the picnic.

Other Designers

Other Herman Miller designers include: **Fritz Baldauf, Jean Beirise** (1988 IBD/*Contract* magazine Gold Award for Ethospace support cabinets), **Aurelio Bevelacqua** (traditional style c. 1927-1930), **Clino Castelli, Freda Diamond, Virginia Dubrucq** (Action Office Series 3 panels), **Richard Holbrook** (1995 NeoCon Best of Show in Seating Category for Ambi Chair), **Dragomir Ivicevic, Harald Jaeger, Wolfgang Mueller-Deisig, Jan Ruhtenberg, Don Shepherd, Edgar Somes, Kathy Stanton** (picnic posters from 1990 on), and the following:

Paul László (1900-1993)

Paul László was born in Budapest, Hungary, into a family involved in the design and manufacture of furniture for three generations. Although he was not considered to have much artistic talent as a youngster, he went on to study architecture in Vienna, Paris, and Berlin. He opened a decorating firm in Vienna in 1923 and in 1927 moved to Stuttgart and established his reputation. In 1936 he moved to Beverly Hills, California and specialized in the design of modern houses and interiors, as well as custom furniture, textiles, and lamps. Clients included Cary Grant, Barbara Hutton, Barbara Stanwyck, Elizabeth Taylor, and Robert Taylor. László designed stores, as well as casinos and showrooms in Howard Hughes's Las Vegas hotels. His

Richard Holbrook; photo *Mark Tuschman*.

Holbrook Ambi Chair; photo 1995 *by Roger Hill*.

Poul Kjaerholm in 1973.

upholstered pieces and table groups for Herman Miller in the late 1940s were among the first of his furniture designs to be produced in the United States; a chair with matching sofa and a circular coffee table were shown in the 1948 Herman Miller catalog.

Fritz Haller (b. 1924)

Born in Solothurn, Switzerland, Fritz Haller became an architect, designer, and town planner. In architecture, he became known for industrial building systems of structural steel: the Maxi system for spanning very wide spaces; the Midi system for medium spans; and the Mini system for short spans. He practiced architecture and urban planning at Solothurn from 1949. In 1960 he designed office systems furniture using interchangeable steel tubes and connectors as frames to support shelves and storage elements. Haller products were introduced in Switzerland in 1964, and from 1964 to 1967 he designed a modular furniture system for USM Haller. The Haller system was distributed in the United States by Herman Miller in 1971,

reintroduced in 1974, and discontinued in 1977. Originally, Herman Miller saw the Haller system as complementing Nelson's designs, but Action Office occupied all of the company's sales and marketing resources, and the Haller system was not given adequate attention. Haller also wrote two books, *Totale Stadt: Ein Modell* in 1968 and *Totale Stadt: Ein globales Modell* in 1975.

Poul Kjaerholm (1929-1980)

A leading designer of Danish Modern furniture, Poul Kjaerholm was trained as a cabinetmaker in a private workshop before studying at the School of Arts and Crafts in Copenhagen from 1949 to 1952. After receiving a degree, he lectured at the school from 1952 to 1956. Beginning in 1955 he designed furniture using a variety of materials — chromed steel, cast aluminum, wood, wicker, leather, marble, plastic, cane, canvas — for E. Kold Christensen. While working as a designer and a teacher, Kjaerholm continued his studies, at the furniture school of the Royal Danish Academy of Fine Arts from 1953 to 1959.

His simple, high quality construction combined comfort with function, and his designs were intended for mass production. The No. 22 steel-framed chair with leather won a grand prize at the Milan Triennale in 1957, one of many international awards. Kjaerholm also won the Year-Prize from the Danish Society of Arts and Crafts in 1957, followed by the Lunning Prize in 1958, the Eckersberg Medal in 1960, the Grand Prix at the XII Milan Triennale in 1960, the Legacy of K.V. Engelhardt in 1965, and the 1972 Annual Prize from the Danish Furniture Manufacturers Association.

In 1973 Herman Miller introduced the Kjaerholm Group in the United States (it had been in production in Denmark from 1955 to 1965), and it remained in production until 1977. According to Hugh De Pree, the company felt that Kjaerholm's products would complement the existing line, and Kjaerholm, an up-and-coming designer, would make a good addition to Herman Miller's design resources. Some of his designs had been developed before being introduced to Herman Miller, while others were developed at the company. Although his products were good, they did not seem to fit well with the systems products of the 1970s. While serving as Director of Furniture Design at the Royal Academy of Fine Arts in Copenhagen he designed several seating items such as high and low easy chairs, a hammock chair, armchair, and a stool.

Verner Panton (b. 1926) Denmark

Born in Denmark, Panton trained at the Odense Technical School and the Royal Danish Academy of Fine Arts in Copenhagen. He worked with Arne Jacobsen's architectural practice from 1950 to 1952. In 1955 he opened his own design office in Bissingen, Switzerland and is credited with designing the first single-form injection-molded plastic chair. He designed for Thonet and for Herman Miller in steel wire, molded plywood and plastic. His single-form plastic chair design of 1959-1960 was produced by Vitra beginning in 1968 under the Herman Miller label. It was made of Baydur, an HR polyurethane foam produced by the Bayer Leverkusen company and varnished in seven colors. It was the first product developed jointly by Vitra

and Bayer Leverkusen to be included in the Herman Miller collection, and it soon became a Pop Art icon. Vitra switched to a more economical thermoplast injection molding in 1970 and continued production until 1979, when the license was returned to Verner Panton. In 1983 Horn GmbH & Co. KG in Rudersberg produced the chair, and it has been made by Vitra since 1990.(von Vegesack 164) The Panton Chair is in the permanent collection of the Museum of Modern Art. Panton's upholstered Cone chair was made from 1958-c. 1966 and the Wire Cone chair from 1959. Pantonova Wire furniture was manufactured from 1961-1966 and the Panton System 1-2-3, consisting of freeform sculptural chairs with three different seat heights in 1974. He also designed lighting, textiles, and carpets. He won the Interior Design Award in 1963 and 1968 in the United States, and the Diploma of Honor at the International Furniture Exhibition in 1969 in Vienna.

Jorgen Rasmussen (b. 1931)

Born in Odense, Denmark, Jorgen Rasmussen graduated from the Royal Academy of Fine Arts in Copenhagen. In 1957 he opened his own architectural office with his twin brother Ib. He has had many important architectural commissions in Denmark and Sweden and in 1960 began to specialize in chair design. His Kevi Chairs for Herman Miller combine economy in design with economy in price, and all chair parts are shipped "knocked-down" and press-fit together without tools on site.

His designs earned him honors and recognition, such as the Neuhausen Prize in 1956, the Royal Academy of Fine Arts Gold Medal in 1959, and the

ID Prize in 1969. He was a professor of Architecture at the Royal Academy of Fine Arts beginning in 1964.

Peter J. Protzmann (b. 1939)

Peter Protzmann was raised in Kansas City, Missouri and earned a B.F.A in Industrial Design from the University of Kansas in 1961. He worked briefly for a large seating company designing stadium, theater, and classroom seating before joining Herman Miller's design and development staff in 1962. Protzmann was involved in the entire design process from concept to production and soon became Senior Designer in the Design and Development Groups.

When Herman Miller introduced the Protzmann Tubular Seating collection in early 1971, the line consisted of a series of low back arm and side chairs intended for the broad commercial and institutional furniture market. The collection grew to include a group of high back arm and side chairs, rockers, tandem seating, high and low back desk chairs, and an office group consisting of a desk, credenza, and storage unit.

Ray Wilkes

Originally from Surrey, England, Ray Wilkes earned a design degree from the Royal College of Art in London in 1961 and was awarded an American Travel Scholarship. He became acquainted with Herman Miller when he worked in New York with George Nelson on special products research and development. He has since worked as a design consultant with companies in England, Europe, and the United States. His contribution to Herman Miller has been in the development of Soft Seating, with special concern for user needs. His knowledge of manufacturing techniques, materials, and design has enabled him to develop chairs of simple classic design, comfort, and improved performance.

Tom Edwards

"My responsibility is for the relationship between an object and the person using it, and psychological comfort is as important to me as physical comfort. I like to use traditional forms, and I want people to be aware of the friendly and familiar aspects of my product. Yet I think fashion adds to the vitality of life, and I want people to see the freshness of my designs."

Tom Edwards received a B.S. in Industrial Design from Kent State University and an M.B.A. from Western Michigan University. He wanted the business degree because he learned that "business principles had as much to do with getting my product to market as any design decision I could make." He designed the Capella chairs for Herman Miller and collaborated on several other significant designs — Action Office system, Action Office Encore system, Action Lab product, Action Factory system, and Ethospace accessories. He was included in the *ID* Annual Design Review for Action Lab in 1982 and won the IBD Product Design award for accessories and lighting in 1978.

Kjaerholm three-seat sofa.

Kjaerholm designs, made by Herman Miller 1973-1977.

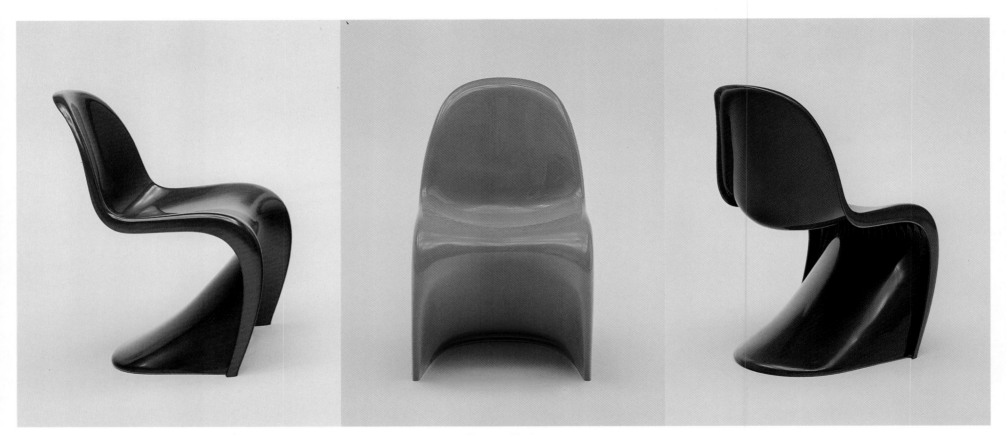

Panton Chair.

Opposite:
Views of the cantilevered
molded plastic Panton Chairs,
designed by Verner Panton in
1959-1960 and in the Herman
Miller collection 1968-1979.

Protzmann Tubular Collection.

1990 Ring Toss picnic poster, by Kathy Stanton.
All Stanton posters are 24 x 38 inches.

1991 Carousel, by Kathy Stanton.
Approximately 1,900 children ten years
old or younger enjoyed the picnic.

199

1992 Tropical Fish, by Kathy Stanton.

1993 Clown, by Kathy Stanton.
More than 7,300 enjoyed the five-hour event.

200

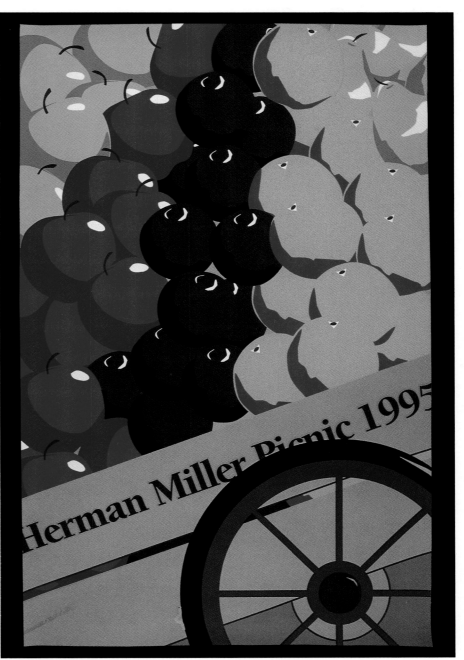

1994 Paints, by Kathy Stanton.
6,800 watched a cabaret performance and a remote control airplane display, and children enjoyed a petting zoo, ponies, and a space walk.

1995 Fruit, by Kathy Stanton.

1996 Brass Band, by Kathy Stanton.

1997 Automobiles, by Kathy Stanton.

202

Herman Miller for the Home

Classics not produced continuously were reissued in 1994 using the same designs and quality of the earlier issues. In a few instances, the Herman Miller for the Home products may vary slightly in materials, finishes, options, dimensions, or other features. For example, endangered wood species such as rosewood are no longer used, and the Molded Plywood Chairs are not made in the variety of colors and materials of the earlier versions. Items produced continuously may also show slight variations, such as the Soft Pad Chair changing from a four-star to a five-star base.

Eames Molded Plywood Dining Chair — Light Ash or Ebony: 1946-1957.
Light ash face veneers and maple inner plies; five-ply seat and back, eight-ply legs and lumbar support; clear coat or ebony; rubber shock mounts. 28-3/4" height, 19-3/8" width.

Eames Molded Plywood Lounge Chair — Light Ash or Ebony: 1946-1957
Light ash face veneers and maple inner plies; five-ply seat and back, eight-ply legs and lumbar support; clear coat or ebony; rubber shock mounts. 26-1/2" height, 22" width.

Eames Molded Plywood Side Chair — Ash or Ebony: 1946-
Five-ply molded plywood; hardwood inner plies and light ash face veneers with either clear coat or ebony finish; bright chrome-plated steel rod base and back brace; rubber shock mounts; nylon glides. 29-1/2" height, 20-1/2" width.

Eames Lounge Chair & Ottoman: 1956-
Seven-ply cherry veneer shell with black leather upholstery; or seven-ply walnut veneer shell with sienna brown leather upholstery; 6-inch-thick urethane foam cushions; swivel mechanism in chair; die cast aluminum back braces, base and ottoman base painted black with bright polished aluminum trim; neoprene shock mounts; adjustable stainless steel glides with rubber bases. 32-3/4" height, 32-3/4" width; ottoman 17-1/4" height, 21-1/2" width.

Eames Aluminum Group Chair: 1958-
Available in choice of seven fabrics; polished die-cast five-star aluminum base, frame, and arms; tubular steel column with enamel finish; layered vinyl cushioning and nylon suspension; seat height adjustment and tilt-swivel mechanism; casters or glides. 33-3/4" max. height (casters), 23" width.

Eames Aluminum Group Lounge Chair: 1958-
Available in choice of seven fabrics; upholstered headrest; polished die-cast aluminum five-star base, frame, and arms; tubular steel column with enamel finish; nylon suspension; 1/2-inch glides. 37" height, 25-3/4" width.

Eames Aluminum Group Ottoman: 1958-
Available in choice of seven fabrics; polished die-cast aluminum four-star base; 1/2-inch glides. 18-1/4" height, 21-1/2 x 21 top.

Eames Soft Pad Chair: 1969-
Available in choice of two leathers, seven fabrics; polished die-cast aluminum five-star base, frame, and arms; tubular steel column with enamel finish; seat height adjustment and tilt-swivel mechanism; nylon suspension; glides or casters. 33-3/4" max. height (casters), 23" width.

Eames Soft Pad Lounge Chair: 1969-
Available in choice of two leathers, seven fabrics; polished die-cast aluminum five-star base, frame, and arms; tubular steel column with enamel finish; tilt-swivel mechanism; nylon suspension; 1/2-inch glides. 36-1/2" height, 26" width.

Eames Soft Pad Ottoman: 1969-
Available in choice of two leathers, seven fabrics; polished die-cast aluminum four-star base, 1/2-inch glides. 19-3/4" height, 21-1/2" square top.

Eames Chaise Lounge: 1968-
Black leather upholstery; 2-inch-thick urethane foam cushions with polyester fiber batting; nylon supporting sling; die-cast aluminum frame coated with egg-plant-colored, electrostatically applied nylon; high-impact black nylon glides. 76-1/2" length, 18" width.

Eames Molded Plywood Folding Screen — Light Ash or Ebony: 1946-1955
Light ash face veneers and strong, lightweight maple inner plies; five-ply; clear coat or ebony; woven polypropylene mesh connects plywood sections. 68" height, 60" width.

Eames Hang-It-All: 1953-1961
Steel rod frame with white powder coat; painted solid maple balls in nine colors; includes hardware package with drywall anchors and screws. 19-3/4" width, 14-5/8 " height.

Eames 2-Seat Sofa (Soft Pad): 1984-
Black leather upholstery; 2-inch-thick urethane-filled cushions; seat cushion bottoms covered with 100% nylon fabric for ventilation; back cushions backed by plywood; solid walnut frame and back; steel braces; die-cast polished aluminum legs and arm supports; nylon glides. 56" length, 33" height.

Eames 3-Seat Sofa (Soft Pad): 1984-
Black leather upholstery; 2-inch-thick urethane-filled cushions; seat cushion bottoms covered with 100% nylon fabric for ventilation; back cushions backed by plywood; solid walnut frame and back; steel braces; die-cast polished aluminum legs and arm supports; nylon glides. 80" length, 33" height.

Eames Sofa Compact: 1954-
Fabric-covered 2 1/2-inch-thick molded urethane foam cushions; choice of seven fabrics; fabric-reinforced rubber webbing seat cushion support; spring support system; steel bar frame and spreaders; chrome-plated legs; adjustable stainless steel glides with rubber base. 72-1/2" length, 35" height.

Eames Molded Plywood Coffee Table — Light Ash or Ebony: 1946-1957
Light ash face veneers and strong lightweight maple inner plies; five-ply top; eight-ply legs; clear coat or ebony. 34" diameter, 15-1/2" height.

Eames Elliptical Table: 1951-1964
Seven-ply Baltic birch core; high-pressure laminate backer on underside; high-pressure laminate top in black or white; wire base with zinc plated or powder coated white or black. 89 x 29-1/2" top, 10" height.

Eames Wire Base Table: 1950-
Seven-ply Baltic birch core; high-pressure laminate backer on underside; high-pressure laminate top in black or white; wire base with zinc plated or powder coated white or black. 15-1/2 x 13-1/4" top, 10" height.

Eames LaFonda Table: 1961-
3/4-inch-thick Perlatto marble or black slate top; polished chrome-plated aluminum base and legs; self-adjusting nylon glides. 30" diameter top, 17-5/8" height.

Eames Round Dining Table (Segmented Base Table): 1964-
1-inch-thick cherry veneer top, black umber tubular steel column, polished aluminum base; column slides into cast aluminum spider screwed into tabletop; bolt running the length of the column secures the base to the tabletop. 54" diameter, 28-1/2" height.

Eames Dining Table (Segmented Base Table): 1964-
Recut light ash or full-cut cherry veneer top; black umber tubular steel columns, polished aluminum base; columns slide into cast aluminum spider screwed into tabletop; bolts running the length of the columns secure the base to the tabletop. 36 x 60", 36 x 72", or 42 x 72" top; 28-1/2" height.

Eames Marble Table — 48" round: 1973-
13/16-inch-thick Italian white marble top, reinforced by white-painted particle board; chrome-plated tubular steel column, polished aluminum base; columns slide into polished aluminum spider screwed into tabletop; bolts running the length of the columns secure the base to the tabletop. 48" diameter, 42" height.

Eames Marble Table — 42"x 72": 1973-
13/16-inch-thick Italian white marble top, reinforced by white-painted particle board; chrome-plated tubular steel column, polished aluminum base; columns slide into polished aluminum spider screwed into tabletop; bolts running the length of the columns secure the base to the tabletop. 72 x 42" top, 42" height.

Eames Walnut Stool (three designs): 1960-
Solid walnut finished in gunstock oil; concave top and bottom surfaces; available in three shapes. 13-1/4" diameter top, 15" height.

Nelson End Tables: 1954-
White or black laminate tabletop and backing; maple veneer edging; polished aluminum or white enamel legs and base assembly, steel-capped glides. Available in three sizes: 17" diameter and 22" height, 28-1/2" diameter and 16-1/2" height, or 28-1/2" diameter and 22" height.

Nelson Miniature Chest, 6-drawer: 1954-1963
Solid teak with rosewood stain on drawer fronts; white powder-coated steel drawer pulls; dividers in middle drawer; white high-pressure laminate top; turned brass feet. 30 x 14", 5-5/8" height.

Nelson Platform Bench 48": 1946-1967
Solid hard maple; ebonized base; metal leveling glides. 48 x 18-1/2" top, 14" height.

Nelson Platform Bench 60": 1946-1967
Solid hard maple; ebonized two-leg base; metal leveling glides. 60 x 18-1/2" top, 14" height.

Nelson Sling Sofa: 1964-
Black leather upholstery; urethane foam cushions; brightly polished chrome-plated tubular steel frame and base; neoprene and reinforced rubber webbing support slings; stainless steel adjustable glides, cushioned in rubber. 87" length, 29-3/4" height.

Noguchi Table: 1948-1973; 1984-
Solid walnut or solid ebonized walnut base; 3/4-inch-thick clear plate glass, with flat polished edges. 50" and 30" sides of top, 15-3/4" height.

Relay Credenza: 1991-
Relay Attached Bookcase w/o Doors: 1991-
Relay Attached Bookcase with Glass Doors: 1991-
Relay Bookcase w/o Doors: 1991-
Relay Bookcase with Solid Doors: 1991-
Relay Bollard: 1991-
Relay Desk: 1991-
Relay Open Work Organizer: 1991-
Relay End Table: 1991-
Relay Folding Screen: 1991-
Relay Puppy: 1991-
Relay Table: 1991-
Relay Teardrop Table: 1991-
Hollington Executive Chair: 1991-
Burdick Dining Table: 1981-
Equa Chair, Fully Upholstered: 1984-
Equa Chair, Split Pad: 1984-
Equa Rocker: 1984-
Proper Chair: 1986-
Scooter: 1986-
Aeron Chair: 1994-
Ambi Chair: 1995-

For the closest retail establishment or for further product information, call (800) 646 4400.

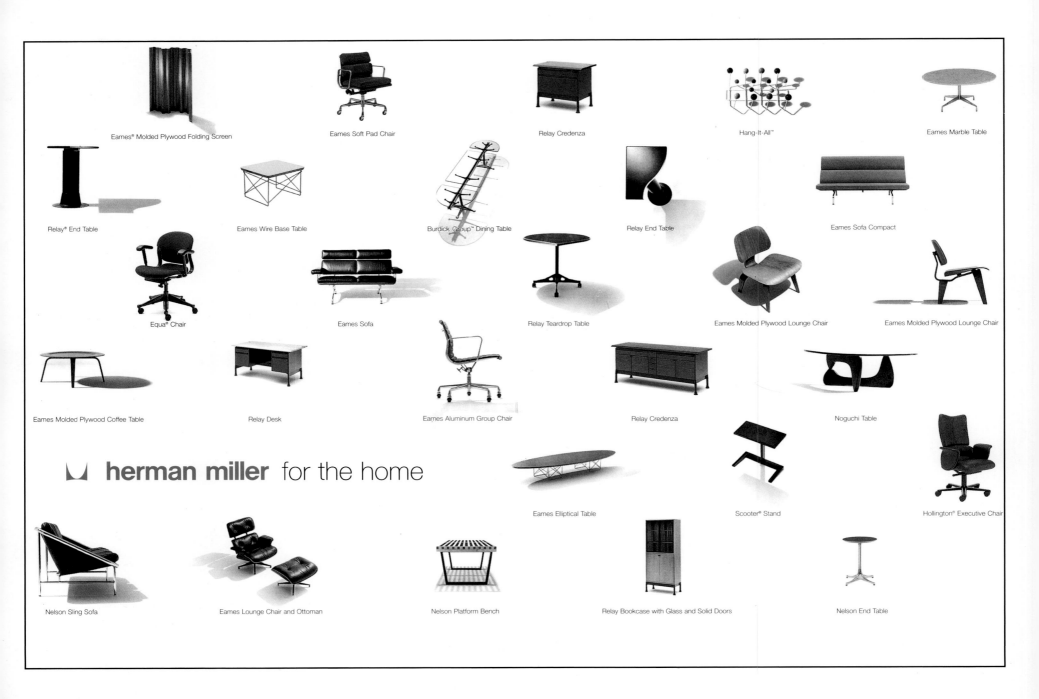

Eames® Molded Plywood Folding Screen

Eames Soft Pad Chair

Relay Credenza

Hang-It-All™

Eames Marble Table

Relay® End Table

Eames Wire Base Table

Burdick Group™ Dining Table

Relay End Table

Eames Sofa Compact

Equa® Chair

Eames Sofa

Relay Teardrop Table

Eames Molded Plywood Lounge Chair

Eames Molded Plywood Lounge Chair

Eames Molded Plywood Coffee Table

Relay Desk

Eames Aluminum Group Chair

Relay Credenza

Noguchi Table

herman miller for the home

Eames Elliptical Table

Scooter® Stand

Hollington® Executive Chair

Nelson Sling Sofa

Eames Lounge Chair and Ottoman

Nelson Platform Bench

Relay Bookcase with Glass and Solid Doors

Nelson End Table

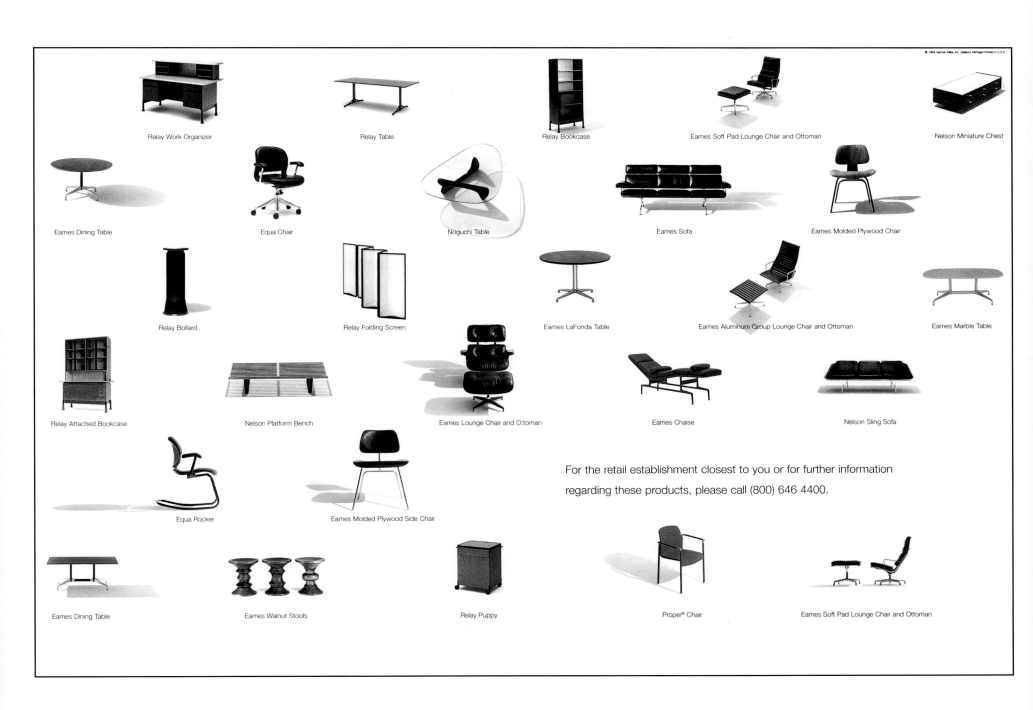

Relay Work Organizer

Relay Table

Relay Bookcase

Eames Soft Pad Lounge Chair and Ottoman

Nelson Miniature Chest

Eames Dining Table

Equa Chair

Noguchi Table

Eames Sofa

Eames Molded Plywood Chair

Relay Bollard

Relay Folding Screen

Eames LaFonda Table

Eames Aluminum Group Lounge Chair and Ottoman

Eames Marble Table

Relay Attached Bookcase

Nelson Platform Bench

Eames Lounge Chair and O:toman

Eames Chaise

Nelson Sling Sofa

Equa Rocker

Eames Molded Plywood Side Chair

For the retail establishment closest to you or for further information regarding these products, please call (800) 646 4400.

Eames Dining Table

Eames Walnut Stools

Relay Puppy

Proper® Chair

Eames Soft Pad Lounge Chair and Ottoman

Selected Bibliography

General Books

Blake, Peter. *No Place Like Utopia: Modern Architecture and the Company We Kept.* New York: Alfred A. Knopf, 1993.

Dormer, Peter. *Design Since 1945.* London: Thames and Hudson, 1993.

Eidelberg, Martin, ed. *Design 1935-1965: What Modern Was.* New York: Harry N. Abrams, 1991.

Emery, Marc. *Furniture by Architects.* New York: Harry N. Abrams, 1983; expanded edition 1988.

Fehrman, Cherie and Kenneth Fehrman. *Postwar Interior Design 1945-1960.* New York: Van Nostrand Reinhold, 1987.

Fiell, Charlotte & Peter. *Modern Furniture Classics Since 1945.* Washington D.C.: AIA Press, 1991.

———. *Modern Chairs.* Kölln, Germany: Taschen, 1993.

Gandy, Charles D. and Susan Zimmermann-Stedham. *Contemporary Classics: Furniture of the Masters.* New York: Whitney Library of Design, 1990 (originally McGraw-Hill, 1981).

Garner, Philippe. *Twentieth-Century Furniture.* New York: Van Nostrand Reinhold, 1980.

Greenberg, Cara. *Mid-Century Modern: Furniture of the 1950s.* New York: Harmony, 1984; reprinted 1995.

Hiesinger, Kathryn B. & George H. Marcus. *Landmarks of Twentieth-Century Design: An Illustrated Handbook.* New York: Abbeville, 1993.

Horn, Richard. *Fifties Style.* New York: Friedman/Fairfax, 1993.

Jackson, Lesley. *The New Look: Design in the Fifties.* New York: Thames Hudson, 1991.

———. *Contemporary Architecture and Interiors of the 1950s.* London: Phaidon, 1994.

Knobel, Lance. *Office Furniture: Twentieth-Century Design.* New York: E. P. Dutton, 1987.

Mang, Karl. *History of Modern Furniture.* New York: Harry N. Abrams, 1978.

Meadmore, Clement. *The Modern Chair: Classics in Production.* New York: Van Nostrand Reinhold, 1975.

Piña, Leslie. *Fifties Furniture.* Atglen, Pennsylvania: Schiffer, 1996.

Pulos, Arthur J. *The American Design Adventure 1940-1975.* Cambridge: MIT Press, 1988.

Sembach, Klaus-Jürgen, et al. *Twentieth-Century Furniture Design.* Köln, Germany: Taschen, n.d.

Sparke, Penny. *Furniture: Twentieth-Century Design.* New York: E. P. Dutton, 1986.

Stimpson, Miriam. *Modern Furniture Classics.* New York: Whitney Library of Design, 1987.

von Vegesack, Alexander et. al. *100 Masterpieces from the Vitra Design Museum Collection.* Weil am Rhein, Germany: Vitra Design Museum, 1996.

Books by or about Herman Miller and its designers:

Abercrombie, Stanley. *George Nelson: the Design of Modern Design.* Cambridge: MIT Press, 1995.

Aldersey-Williams, Hugh and Geoff Hollington. *Hollington Industrial Design.* London: Architecture Design and Technology Press, 1990.

Caplan, Ralph. *The Design of Herman Miller.* New York: Whitney Library of Design, 1976.

———. *Connections: The Work of Charles and Ray Eames.* exhibition catalog. Los Angeles: Frederick S. Wight Art Gallery, 1976.

Cruikshank, Jeffrey L. and Clark Malcolm. *Herman Miller, Inc.: Buildings and Beliefs.* Washington D.C.: A.I.A. Press, 1994.

De Pree, Hugh. *Business as Unusual.* Zeeland, Michigan: Herman Miller, 1986.

Herman Miller Furniture Co. *The Herman Miller Collection.* catalogs. Zeeland, Michigan: Herman Miller Furniture Co., 1948, 1950, 1952 (also reprinted New York: Acanthus Press, 1995), 1955/56 (also reprinted Atglen, Pennsylvania: Schiffer Publishing, 1998).

Herman Miller, Inc. *Action Office System.* Zeeland, Michigan: Herman Miller, Inc., 1984.

———. *Reference Points.* Zeeland, Michigan, Herman Miller, 1984.

———. *Burdick Group Pages.* product brochure. Zeeland, Michigan, Herman Miller, 1992.

———. *Herman Miller for the Home.* product catalog. Zeeland, Michigan: Herman Miller, 1995.

———. *Herman Miller Pricebooks: Seating & Furniture.* Zeeland, Michigan: Herman Miller, 1995.

———. *Herman Miller Catalog.* Zeeland, Michigan: Herman Miller, 1996.

———. *Marigold Lodge.* Zeeland, Michigan, Herman Miller, n.d.

Hunter, Sam. *Isamu Noguchi.* New York: Abbeville, 1978.

Kirkham, Pat. *Charles and Ray Eames: Designers of the Twentieth Century.* Cambridge: MIT, 1995.

Nelson, George. *Chairs.* New York: Whitney, 1953; reprinted New York: Acanthus, 1994.

———. *Display.* New York: Whitney, 1953.

———. *Storage.* New York: Whitney, 1954.

———. *Problems of Design.* New York: Whitney, 1957.

———. *George Nelson on Design.* New York: Whitney Library of Design, 1979.

———. *Changing the World.* University of Michigan, 1987.

Neuhart, John, Marilyn Neuhart, & Ray Eames. *Eames Design.* New York: Harry N. Abrams, 1991.

Propst, Robert. *The Office: A Facility Based on Change.* Zeeland, Michigan: Herman Miller, Inc., 1968.

———. *Action Office: The System that Works for You.* Ann Arbor, Michigan: Herman Miller Research Corp., 1978.

Propst, Robert, et. al. *The Senator Hatfield Office Innovation Project.* Ann Arbor, Michigan: Herman Miller Research Corp., 1977.

Renwick Gallery. *A Modern Consciousness: D. J. De Pree, Florence Knoll.* exhibit catalog. Washington D. C: Smithsonian Institution Press, 1975.

University of Illinois. *William Stumpf Industrial Design.* exhibition brochure. Urbana-Champaign: University of Illinois, 1995.

Articles

"A Conversation with George Nelson." *Industrial Design* (April 1969): 76-77.

Berman, Ann. "Herman Miller — Influential Designs of the 1940s and 1950s." *Architectural Digest* (September 1991): 34-40.

Brenson, Michael. "Isamu Noguchi, the Sculptor, Dies at 84." *The New York Times* (December 31, 1988): obituary.

Caplan, Ralph. "Caplan on Nelson." *I.D.* (January February 1992): 76-83.

"Designers in America: Part 3." *Industrial Design* (Oct. 1972): 30-31.

"Furniture Best of Category: Aeron Chair." *I.D. Annual Design Review 1995* (July/August 1995).

Gingerich, Owen. "A Conversation with Charles Eames." *The American Scholar.* (Summer 1977): 326-337.

"Herman Miller for the Home." *Interior Design* (December 1993).

McQuade, Walter. "Charles Eames Isn't Resting on His Chair." *Fortune* (February 1975): 96-100, 144-145.

Nelson, George. "The Furniture Industry." *Fortune 35* (January 1947): 106-111.

———. "Business and the Industrial Designer." *Fortune* (July 1949): 92-98.

———. "Modern Furniture." *Interiors.* (July 1949): 77-89.

———. "Design, Technology, and the Pursuit of Ugliness." *Saturday Review* (October 2, 1971): 22-25.

Ostergard, Derek and David Hanks. "Gilbert Rohde and the Evolution of Modern Design 1927-1941." *Arts Magazine* (October 1981).

———. "Gilbert Rohde: The Herman Miller Years." 7-page typescript in Herman Miller Archives, n.d.

Pearlman, Chee. "Machine for Sitting." *I.D.* (September/October 1994).

"Royal Gold Medal for Architecture 1979: The Office of Charles and Ray Eames." 12-page packet, April 1979.

Schwartz, Bonnie. "2 Chairs, 2 Processes." *Metropolis* (May 1996).

Slesin, Suzanne. "George H. Nelson, Designer of Modernist Furniture, Dies." *The New York Times* (March 4, 1986): D26, obituary.

"Storage Wall." *Life* (January 1945): 64-71.

Sudjic, Deyan. "Playfulness." *Blueprint* (October 1994): 29-36.

Tetlow, Karin. "Dock 'N' Roll." *Interiors* (September 1990): 146-151.

"3 Chairs/ 3 records of the design process." *Interiors* (April 1958): 118-152.

"25: Year of Appraisal." *Interiors* (November 1965): 128-161.

Walker Art Center "Nelson, Eames, Girard, Propst: the Design Process at Herman Miller." exhibit catalog. *Design Quarterly 98/99* (1975): 1-64.

Wierenga, Debra, ed. "Design and the Office in Transition — Part I: A Conversation with George Nelson." *Ideas* (November 1979): 1-20.

Archives

Herman Miller Archives. Photographs and written material on designers, products, and the company. Contributors to the database containing material used in this project include Linda Folland, Hugh De Pree, Barbara Hire, Will Poole, and Bob Viol. Quotes by designers not attributed to other sources are from the "Designer Bio" promotional sheets produced by Herman Miller.

Index

Value Guide

Furniture is different from other decorative arts with regard to pricing, especially because condition ranges from the rare perfect piece to those showing degrees of wear and use. Furniture was used in someone's home or office — some pieces more lovingly than others — so prices will be affected by condition or restoration. In addition, each region of the country will have a market directed by supply and demand, by individual tastes, and by fashions or trends. In the case of modern furniture, such as these Herman Miller classics, the major coastal cities, plus other centers for modernism such as Chicago and Detroit, generally have the largest and most established markets, and perhaps the highest prices. Large European and Japanese cities have also shown keen interest in American modernism. Auctions also help to guide or set prices, but auctions are events, and once the lots are sold, similar examples at future sales may bring very different prices. In addition, Herman Miller has continuously produced several of these classic designs and has reissued others. The 1994 Herman Miller for the Home collection features these plus later additions that have already become classics in their own right.

With this in mind, it is clear that any price guide for modern furniture is apt to be uneven, to say the least, and *neither the author nor the publisher can be responsible for any outcomes from consulting this guide.* The only guarantee about this or any other value guide is that some readers will buy and/or sell outside of the listed range. That's a fact. Our intent is to give a general idea of some typical prices that similar items have recently sold for and might sell for again. It will also help to distinguish the relatively common from the rare pieces. Most of the items listed are by Eames and Nelson — there are probably more of Herman Miller's Eames and Nelson designs available on the American market than all other modern designers combined. Prices are in United States dollars, and a range is given to account for different secondary market sources as well as for different finishes, sizes, or other options originally offered for some of the designs. Prices given are for early issues; recent Herman Miller for the Home items, labeled as such, may list for much higher OR much lower prices than comparable items on the secondary market. It is assumed that pieces are in excellent condition with reasonable wear but no damage. Of course, the pristine example in near mint condition should command a higher price, and there is always the "sleeper" that is worth more than its price tag. Those are surprises that all collectors hope to find. In the meantime, I hope that this book brings you enjoyment and provides information that can improve the odds.

Page	Item	Price
p. 22	Splint	$300-400
p. 26	Table	$2,000-4,000
	Chair	$3,000-4000
	Stool	$1,500-2,000
p. 27	Table	$2,000-4,000
	Chair	$3,000-4,000
p. 29	DCW/LCW	$600-800
p. 30	EC 110/LCM	$100-400
p. 31	LCW	$600-800
p. 32	LCM slunk skin	$800-1,000
p. 33	CTM	$900-1,200
	Square	$600-800
	LCM	$150-250
	CTW	$900-1,200
p. 35	Chair	$150-200
p. 37	Chair	$150-250
p. 38	Chair	$150-250
pp. 44-45	Stacking	$75-150
	Swivel	$200-300
p. 47	Armshell	$300-500
pp. 48-49	LaFonda	$200-400
pp. 50-51	Shell/Sec.	$200-400
p. 52	Table	$800-1,200
	Chair	$150-250
p. 53	Table	$600-800
	Chair	$150-250
p. 54	Chair	$100-300
p. 55	Rocker	$600-900
	Chair	$100-300
p. 57	Sofa	$1,000-2,000
p. 58	Lounge & Ott	$2,000-3,000
p. 62	Management	$300-500
	Lounge & Ott	$800-1,000
p. 64	Aluminum	$300-700
p. 65	Lounge	$400-600
	Time-Life	$700-900
p. 66	Management	$700-900
	Lounge & Ott.	$1,000-1,400
p. 67	Chaise	$1,500-2,500
p. 68	Sofa	$2,000-3,000
p. 69	LaFonda	$400-600
	Round Seg.	$300-500
	Rectangular	$500-800
p. 70	Table	$300-800
p. 71	Surf	$2,000-3,000
	Marble	$1,000-2,000
	Wire Base	$300-500
p. 72	Stool	$600-800
p. 73	Storage Unit	
	100-150 series	$1,000-3,000
	200-250 series	$3,000-6,000
	400 series	$8,000-12,000
p. 74	Screen	$2,000-4,000
p. 75	Hang-It-All	$800-1,200
p. 81	Bubble	$150-350
p. 83	EOG	$700-1,000 each unit
p. 84	EOG	$1,000-1,500
p. 85	Table	$300-600
p. 86	End Table	$100-300
p. 87	Pedestal	$500-800
p. 88	Writing	$6,000-10,000
p. 89	Square Coffee	$400-700
p. 90	Round Coffee	$600-800
p. 91	Table	$800-1,200
p. 92	48"-102" Bench	$500-1,500
p. 93	Cabinet	$600-800 each unit
	Cabinet w legs	$800-1,200 each
p. 94	Cabinet	$600-800 each
p. 95	Miniature	$1,500-2,500
p. 96	Miniature	$1,500-2,500
p. 97	Bed	$1,200-2,200
p. 98	Daybed	$1,200-2,200
p. 99	Thin Edge	$800-1,200 each unit
p. 100	Chaise	$3,000-5,000
p. 101	High Back	$1,500-2,500
p. 103	Angle Frame	$400-600
p. 104	Knock Down	$400-600
p. 105	Kangaroo	$1,800-2,500
p. 106	Pretzel	$2,000-3,000
p. 108	Coconut	$1,500-2,500
p. 109	Flying Duck	$1,000-1,500
p. 110	Marshmallow	$9,000-12,000
p. 112	Swaged	$600-900
p. 114	Roll Top	$1,500-2,000
p. 115	Roll Top	$1,500-2,000
p. 116	Catenary	$1,000-1,500
p. 117	Catenary	$1,000-1,500
p. 118	Sling	$2,000-3,000
p. 119	Cube	$600-800
p. 120	Modular	$500-800 each unit
p. 122	Fin Table	$4,000-5,000
	Fin Stool	$3,000-5,000
p. 123	Table	$1,500-2,500
p. 128	Dining Set	$3,000-4,000
p. 129	Seating	$2,000-3,000
	Bookcase	$1,500-2,000
	Table	$1,000-1,500
p. 130	Rohde	$1,000-1,500 each unit
p. 131	Table	$500-700
	Vanity	$2,500-3,500
	Lounge	$1,000-1,500
p. 132	Cabinet	$2,000-3,000 each
p. 136	Ottoman, Table	$500-1,500
p. 137	Seating	$1,500-3,000
p. 194	Sofa	$800-1,200
p. 195	Lounge	$600-800
	Sofa	$800-1,200
	Chairs	$300-600
pp. 196-197	Chairs	$150-300
p. 198	Tubular	$300-500